AT A
TIME

ONE DAY AT A TIME

*The search for hope
through trauma*

REBECCA ANDREW-CROWE

BROWN
DOG
BOOKS

Published under licence by Brown Dog Books and
The Self-Publishing Partnership, 7 Green Park Station, Bath BA1 1JB

www.selfpublishingpartnership.co.uk

ISBN 978-1-78545-258-1

Cover design by Kevin Rylands

Internal design by Jenny Watson Design

Printed and bound in the UK

With thanks

Ultimately to The Lord, thank you for guiding me.
Simply, you saved my soul.

David, thank you. For everything. You have supported me throughout my whole life. Thank you for loving me and thank you for making me believe again. All the times I have been unsure, you have been certain. You provided faith when I lost mine. Thank you.

Zac and Brioni, you have both been my true inspiration, my reasons for fighting and my ultimate pride and joy. Thank God for you both. Your excitement and zest for life have been hard to keep up with. Thank you for letting me be part of your amazing life's journeys.

Written from The Watch Tower

One Day at a Time
_____

CONTENTS

1

Preface

5

LIFE CAN WAIT

29

DISCONNECTED

55

FRAGILE

65

NOT ME, NOT I

73

IN MY OWN TIME

79

BELIEVE AGAIN

95

RIGHT HERE IN MY HEART

110

NO CRY FOR HELP

113

*Agencies which provide
support and information*

PREFACE

"Remembering that I'll be dead soon is the most important tool I've ever encountered to help me make the big choices in life. Because almost everything – all external expectations, all pride, all fear of embarrassment or failure – these things just fall away in the face of death, leaving only what is truly important. Remembering that you are going to die is the best way I know to avoid the trap of thinking you have something to lose. You are already naked. There is no reason not to follow your heart."

Steve Jobs

One Day at a Time is a journey; one that was to become a way of life. It is the untold story of the mental struggle and of a cancer that took hold of my mind and changed my world as I had once known it. It's not easy to tell this story. Not easy to tell you that I was robbed of my joy, my hope and nearly took my own life. When I attend my usual doctor's appointments, words appear on that highlighted summary screen, words that apparently sum up by behaviour, my feelings. I know the doctor sees them and automatically assumes a judgement of understanding prior to knowing anything further on my part.

Mental Breakdown. Attempted Suicide.

The words do not even begin to say anything about why, what happened, what caused it. The words say more than enough yet so very little. I guess I never thought I would have that wording on my screen, and since it appeared I have spent a lot of time thinking about it, what it actually means. Is there no such thing other than a collection of symptoms? A trigger in life? The way you react? Is it really an illness or an unfortunate set of circumstances, to then suffer twice from? The real question of psychology: should it be not what's wrong, but what happened?

Kindness is essential to mental peace. Kindness to everyone, starting with ourselves. Compassion, kindness, and love. The recipe for life. A story of support, hope, and courage to live on. *One Day at a Time* is a journey which later became a way of life. A way of living, simply the only way to live. A search for personal freedom through trauma, to recovery, to a different 'me'. This is for every 'Tommy and Gina' out there. For each and every one of you who has felt so fearful to live.

For Brioni
For Zac
For Michael
For Marie
For Kevin
For Kym
possibly for YOU

And finally for me, Becki, the Optical Consultant, the mother of two, the girl with a terrible case of mistaken identity

If you're going through hell, keep going

I don't care how you recover. I simply care that you do

With love, light, and hope

Rebecca Andrew-Crowe

*"My entire life can be described in one sentence:
it didn't go as planned, and that's OK."*

Rachel Wolchin

———————

"When we can't dream any longer we die."

Emma Goldman

LIFE CAN WAIT

It doesn't really matter what took me there that night, the reasons behind why I walked into that A and E department late one evening. All I know is that it could have been any one, any one of us. For a million different reasons at any given day or time. The trouble is, it wasn't you, or the girl you know from work, or the bloke across the road. It was me.

The rain fell heavy that evening. The sort of rain that soaks you to the skin. It had been miserable all day with no signs of letting up. My favourite type of weather – I always loved the thought of sitting in the bay window at home with the log fire burning watching the rain from the safe and warm indoors. Would love it in the evening when a storm came in. I found it therapeutic and cuddled up with a hot chocolate and a blanket. Just pure bliss. The wind was building; it was one of those days where you hold on to your car door when you get in or out in case you lose it. Absolutely freezing even with three layers on. The day had been a blur, but this wasn't uncommon. I guess most days were. Home to work, work to kids, kids' hobbies, home. Life, right? The normal existence of a working mum, not enough hours in the day. Nothing abnormal and nothing that I wasn't quite apt at. I was a master juggler, years of experience under my belt. If anyone knew how to juggle many things at once it was me. This had been the case for years, and today was nothing more than just a normal weekday. I loved the buzz, the organization and the challenge of life; nothing really phased me. I thrived on logistical nightmares and dashing here, there and everywhere. What was different was me, how I felt, how I behaved and how I reacted. Something had happened. That something isn't important to this story now, but how it has altered my life since is.

I sat in my parked car down some quiet residential street with the engine running and the heater on full blast. The rain pounded on the windscreen. The sound of the engine drowned out my cries. The reflection of the streetlight, blurred through the rain drops, was hard to make out through the tears that fell down my face. Utterly distraught, I was inconsolable and absolutely breaking my heart. I hadn't planned to be here, it most certainly was not on my agenda of the day. I had skipped a badminton class and not even messaged in to say I couldn't make it. Dropped the kids off home, they along with my husband assumed I had gone, I guess. I hadn't told them otherwise and they didn't ask. I rushed out in a hurry avoiding making eye contact with David. Luckily the kids were upstairs arguing who was first in the shower so I shouted up a quick goodbye and left. The tears had come all day and caught me out on a few occasions but now they just wouldn't stop. Throughout the morning I had tried to be as composed as possible, holding conversations and going about the daily tasks, but it was merely a physical function. Tears crept in at every possible chance. 'You alright today, Bex?' I got asked by several curious colleagues.

I avoided eye contact, nodded and looked busy. I was busy being lost. Just focused, that's all. Focused on the job, there was no time for the polite conversation today.

Driving the kids home, my eyes were streaming. Cautiously I would wipe them away and tell myself to focus. *Focus woman, pull yourself together.* For the first time ever, I was struggling to compose myself; me, struggling to pull myself together. It was unheard of, this never happened. Not me, not I. Cutting conversations short as I felt tears building up, every little thing in this normal day was a challenge like I had never known it before. My mind was elsewhere. Where, I really am not quite sure although I believed I had done a pretty good job at pulling the tasks of the day off. I knew myself I was incredibly fragile.

I sat there so very frightened. Sheer panic and terror totally controlled me. Struggling to breathe, a tight pain crushed my chest and I battled with feeling like I was going to faint to then the overwhelming urge to throw up. Get some air, I told myself. Some fresh air. I swung the car door open. The rain was pounding down heavy and as I went to get out of the car I couldn't find the strength to stand. Sitting on the edge of the driver's seat, leading forward with my head in my hands and my legs out in the rain. My feet firmly placed on the shiny wet tarmac, slippery. *Don't stand, just breathe, Becki. Just breathe.* No, too cold. I was freezing. Shaking, I pulled my legs back inside, soaked to the skin. So very frightened, but what of? Now, I had never been a successful runner so when people say they hit a wall I could never really comprehend that. Always wondered what they meant. After watching 'Run Fat Boy, Run' it clicked. I loved that movie. The humour and the story. Easy to watch and the visual wall he hit when he lost all strength, motivation, and energy, where he just could not go on. That is how I felt. I had hit a wall. A wall, a block aid, something that represented a point of not being able to take any more. Whatever it was, I had hit it hard. Noticeably to me, and most worrying wasn't the fact that I felt physically ill with my chest, nor was it the constant flow of tears that I had lost control over. It was my thinking. I have always, always been a positive thinker. A believer, a dreamer. A person who always believed in endless opportunities and ways around the most improbable situations. I had hope. Hope for everything. And not only did I have hope, I gave hope. Friends would often come to me when things were hard for them, family members and even patients I worked with would say my personality was infectious for a positive outlook and spin on things. No matter what it was in life, there was always hope for a more favourable outcome, hope for good news, hope for any possibility. But there was none, no hope at all. Sitting in my car I had lost all hope for my future, my direction and most importantly for my search for peace. I had long since felt peace. What I felt was lost. Completely and utterly lost, yet surrounded in life. I had never felt so alone and detached from those who I loved.

Phone David and tell him how you feel.

You are so weak it's pathetic

Becki, go and tell someone and get some help, then life can get back to how you know it.

Get a grip. If you can't cope then do something about it, but don't drag others down with you.

Find the words Becki, tell someone, no one could cope with this alone

I'm so scared.

I stood in the queue at the reception. Second place in line. Behind the red line on the floor, NHS policy to maintain confidentiality and dignity of those in front declaring their ailments over the counter to a receptionist inputting it all into the system. The system that prioritizes you over another based on symptoms entered, and then triage nurse's quick five-minute assessment before the wait begins. The waiting room held a few solemn-faced people. Not that I expected a happy bunch, I mean, who really wants to be hanging out at a hospital? Hardly a fun night out. The wall-mounted TV flashed with repetitive adverts about washing your hands; the latest flu vaccine now available; ask your GP; and the waiting list time of three to four hours to be seen. There were no visible injuries apart from a young lad with a busted nose. He sat in the corner with his mates loudly chatting about the incident that led him here. Everyone else didn't look immediately ill. They could have been waiting for family of course, or as we all know there are many pains and illnesses that can't be seen, but they didn't look in need of physical help. This made me feel slightly more like I would fit it. I didn't look ill either, so I would blend in with them. I could be waiting for family, no one would know. *Deep breaths, Becki, you have done the right thing, you're doing the right thing.* Now it was my turn. The male receptionist looked up and beckoned me over. I was stuck. My feet rooted to the floor. My legs were so heavy I could not move them. For the longest moment ever, I was frozen solid. Mentally I was unable to function. Never before could I not think straight. *Turn around and go, Becki. What on earth are you doing? Leave now, you've already made a fool out of yourself.* Aware only of my inability to move and my fighting internal thoughts, I was disconnected from the world outside. I featured physically in it but that was it. Glued to the floor and mentally zoned in on the red waiting line, that vision became a thought process. If I crossed the line, I would never return. What would be over that red line? Safety? It had been a long time since I felt safe. I was quite surprised to find the receptionist standing next to me with his hand out gentling reaching for my arm. "Are you alright, madam? Can I help you?" I hadn't realized I had been crying quite so much. He was a blur, no definite lines to his shape. I wondered if I was awake or not. A bit like that fainting feeling, where reality fades into a questionable dream. His touch snapped me back into the hospital. I looked up suitably embarrassed. *Stay or go, Becki.* If it wasn't for him telling me what to do that moment I would have pivoted and left. "Come and sit down through here and you can tell me what you're here for." *Follow the instruction, Becki.* An order, a direction. I needed to be told what to do. I was unable to think clearly enough myself. It was too late. My thinking was broken. I needed the direction of someone else's orders. He led me into a quiet corridor with a row of seats. He fetched a square box of tissues to me and sat next to me with a paper clipboard and pen. I told him my name and answered the questions, trying to compose myself through every response. I found myself stammering. Stuttering and stammering when I spoke, I was too nervous to function. It was when he asked me what was wrong that I surprised myself by saying it so easily. I had no conscious thoughts of trusting him, to a bloke, I had never met, I blurted out the words between a persistently heavy flow of tears, a force of nature that would just not stop, powerful and unstoppable that carried my soul with each one.

"I want to die now. I cannot live like this any longer. I do not trust myself not to take my own life."

You've told him, you said it, you will get some help now.

You stupid sod, fancy saying that. What will he think of you? Admitting you're suicidal, shame on you!

No, you recognized you needed help and was brave, Becki.

You should have just bloody killed yourself. Waste of space.

You don't really feel like that, you know you will be at work tomorrow, pull yourself together.

Look what you've done now.

Just forget about it, pretend it didn't happen

Wasting people's time. Go and jump off a bridge and get it over with.

I didn't look at his face when I said it. I held a tissue in my hands, I could barely see it but I could feel it. And as the tears poured down my cheeks, I focused on the fibres of that tissue. That was my connection to the physical world I was in. Pulling it apart between my thumbs, the fabric fibres tore easily under pressure. That tissue, easily broken, which, when torn, can never be reconnected. Intangible. That was my world, falling apart, incapable of being perceived by the sense of touch. It was the first time I had said it out loud. Saying things makes them real. When you just think things, even if they are powerful things, it's a world of your own that's protected. Bringing them out into the open makes it a different sort of reality. To openly admit to something that shames you, whatever it is, isn't easy. I wasn't proud of how I felt, I was ashamed. We spend our lives trying to hide our imperfections. I couldn't decide whether walking into A and E was a saving grace or a moment of pure madness. The bloke didn't say much more. He muttered something about staying where I was and he would get a nurse to see me. Inconsolable, I cried and cried and there was absolutely no attempting to pull myself together. My heart raced like I had never known it before. I was past caring about who saw me. In an openly public but relatively quiet corridor, I sat there and sobbed. I did not care. That function wasn't in me to feel anymore. I was disorientated, lost, desperate and had reached my limit in life. I was conscious of a few people walking past me and was thankful that nobody spoke. The reception chap returned and said I was on the list to be seen and to wait where I was. I didn't move from that seat. In fact, I tried to make myself smaller. I pulled by legs up to my chest to feel more compact, safe and secure. Maybe I could disappear. I would like to disappear. I buried my head in my knees and blocked out the external world. But I could not block out the world I was really in. My reality was most present, and a whirlwind of thoughts occupied every single second of a journey. Although I was physically stationary, mentally I travelled very far, into an incredibly dark place. Thousands of tears later I could not bring myself back up from such depths I never knew existed.

"Rebecca, come with me"

I can't tell you how long I was sat in that corridor for. The sense of time had lost me. The female nurse who spoke to me must have repeated herself at least three times before I was mentally present back at the hospital. I hadn't been asleep, but I wasn't fully awake either. I reached for my handbag and stood up to follow her. My legs were no longer heavy, but weak. I wondered if they would carry my weight. I was so very cold and my hands trembled. Toilet – I needed the toilet. The nurse directed me to the ladies. Surprisingly, when I looked in the mirror my physical self was still there. Apart from swollen eyes, red puffy cheeks and messy hair that had been thrown up into a loose bun, I was still there. Still in my work clothes, smartly tailored navy trousers, an ecru-pleated ruffle top hidden by a navy striped jacket, a silk scarf and polished leather ankle boots. I was still that woman who went to work that morning, a mother with two beautiful children at home, a wife with a loving husband. Yet I was not. Looking at my reflection was like an out-of-body experience. What I saw I recognized, but I didn't feel. I was no longer that person who looked back at me. There was a separation between my mind and body. I must have passed several patients, people waiting for their loved ones and medical staff just going to the ladies, yet I couldn't make out anyone's face. But I knew I had passed physical bodies. What would they think had happened to me? What was the reason I looked so visibly distressed? Had I received awful news? Could anyone see past this physical exterior and know what was really happening?

The department was large and very busy. The murmur of chatter was consistent; a young child shrieking from afar; fast-paced staff walking around with notes and serious faces; a unit buzzing with life; a cleaner sweeping the floors; and family members being escorted to their loved ones. I could overhear a woman on her phone updating someone about her loved one's progress. An accident at work, awaiting x-ray, possible fracture. Glancing at the opposite cubical there lay a man on a stretcher. He had obviously been brought in by ambulance. His leg looked awful on blood-stained sheets. A trauma injury, maybe. He looked in pain but I could tell the drugs he had been given were working. Any movement made his face screw up, but then that dazed half-asleep-look when he remained still took over. I wished I was him. I wished my pain was visible with a valid reason for all to see. They knew what was wrong with him – a broken leg, a fractured tibia, a damaged muscle. Whatever it was, it could be fixed. They knew what they had to do and they could begin to sort it immediately. From diagnostics to full treatment, that chap would get answers, an outcome, and an understanding quite quickly of his injuries and his future. He may have operations, a plate even put in if it was a nasty break, scars for the rest of his life, war wounds to show his grandkids, tablets he would take would help him. And within

6 to 12 weeks he would know the pain would be gone and the healing nearly complete. But not me.

Sitting in the cubical waiting for a doctor to assess me, I felt uneasy, uncomfortable. What was I doing here? What would I say when the doctor came in? I had no physical wounds to show him or her. What did I want? To stay in the hospital? To be given drugs? I did not know what I wanted. I did not know what I was asking for nor why I had come. What help is there for someone who can't explain anything other than life is too scary to live anymore? Dying now seemed the only answer. I had lost all control over my life as I knew it. I really didn't want to be admitted. I didn't want anything but me back. I wanted to feel like I could cope with living. To trust myself that I could live on and not have to die because I couldn't face life anymore. I wanted to be free and feel peace. I wanted to feel those around me and connect again. I was so very tired. Exhausted from the emotional state I had been, it seemed as though months of build-up emotions came out in that cubical. An endless flow of tears.

I was always one for following instructions. I guess that's how I was brought up. Do what is asked of you. If you Google 'suicidal thoughts' it quite clearly states to ask for help immediately: see your GP or go to the nearest hospital. I know it states on the boxes of certain medications that if you feel worse then seek help immediately. I remembered reading that once, a box of two diazepams given to me by my doctor. A few years back I had a spate of MRI scans for one thing or another. The first time in that tunnel was the first time I had ever actually felt scared. I could touch the ceiling with my nose. I could literally see my breath condense centimetres above my eyes, and realizing I was trapped with no escape sent me into a nervous frenzy of twitching, uncontrolled shaking and breathing so fast I thought my chest would explode. "Focus on the music," they told me via the speaker. Hell, I couldn't even make out the music never mind focus on it. I was focusing on the lack of air, the straps that held me to the table to keep my spine in place, not any music. My mind was on high alert, trapped with no way out. It was, quite simply, terrifying. I vowed never to get back into a machine like it. That was until the doctor phoned me up and said the scan was inconclusive due to movement on my behalf. How do you expect me to stay still when I am panicking, I asked the doctor. His answer was simple, "I have the perfect tablet for you, Becki. This will get you sorted." So, I read the little information sheet whilst I waited for my next scan. It worked very well and I was thankful for that. A wonderful invention, I joked with friends. Who knew these existed?! I sure glad I had come to find out.

When hope is gone, it destroys us. No matter what happens in life, there must be some hope. I tried to compose myself. Told myself I had done the right thing, I was safe from myself for now. I was sensible. I hadn't lost it all completely, I had made a sensible decision. *See, Becki, you can think for yourself. You recognized you needed help and asked for it.* Maybe they could give me one of those diazepam tablets I'd had before. Maybe that's all I needed, just get me back on track. If I can stop my mind from racing I may be able to think straight, and if I can think straight, I can function, and life can go on. There you go, I told myself, hope. That's what I need. That is what I would ask for when the doctor came in.

I scrolled down my contacts list on my phone. 374 contacts. 374 people who knew me, who would possibly help me if I asked. Yet I had never felt so alone. I scrolled up and down. OK, so not necessarily 374 people whom I knew well. Business contacts, work colleagues, tenants, dentist, doctor, hairdresser, my children's friend's mums who I didn't really know but liaised with every so often to aid the children's social lives, close family, annoying family, distant family who make contact every Christmas, friends who you would see occasionally, friends who you can be real in front of and those that you can't. There were some good people on that list. I knew that. I knew the ones who genuinely cared, I knew I was lucky to have their names stored in my phone. I also knew however that no one could help me with this. This indescribable torment that I was secretly living in. I couldn't even explain this to myself, how on earth would I begin to ask for help when I wasn't quite sure what I was asking for? Who could possibly see what was going on internally?

My favourites list: my husband, and my children. They had little yellow stars next to their names. It made me smile as I never listed them under their actual names. Instead, I used characters that represented them which came from fond family memories. My daughter was known as 'Cindy Loo' from one of our favourite movies, 'The Grinch'. Such a sweet, kind-hearted little girl trapped in a society celebrating greed. My daughter was like that little girl, always looking for the good in everyone. I stared at the three most important names in my life on one small screen. Everything right there, a simple touch away. A reason to live, my world. So close I could touch them but so far away that they were unreachable.

After many tormented hours waiting on a stretcher, my experience of life in the mindset I was in was pure frightening. Grasping at anything to tell myself I was safe. Physically momentarily maybe, but mentally I was not safe from myself. Curled up as small as possible I battled with different versions of reality. I longed for my mind to stop. Just stop. Just shhh. But my mind did everything but silence. A woman appeared from nowhere which once again brought me back into my physical reality. Very business-like, tailored trousers, fitted shirt, file and pen in hand. She was austere and I immediately felt ashamed. She had her NHS ID lanyard around her neck. I couldn't quite make out her name but that feeling of dread overwhelmed me. Her attitude was incredibly formal and certainly not one that put you at ease. Ironically, that was me this morning, dressed smartly, focused. I found it strange how an outward perspective image could be so very wrong and hide something internally so different so well.

"Rebecca, I need you to sit up and answer a few questions." Just like I was told, I did. She was weighing me up straight away, how I moved, how I spoke, piecing my life together from the image she saw before her. I answered everything as best I could. No, I hadn't had a mental health assessment before. No, I had never self-harmed. Yes, I had a busy life. No, I don't always sleep well. No, I didn't always eat properly. The questions went on and on and they were all irrelevant. I couldn't understand in my mind why these things were important. What did it matter if I enjoyed watching TV? Or if I had taken a vacation in the last 12 months? She went to on tell me she wasn't a doctor. The doctors in A and E were too busy with trauma injuries, run off their feet, she said, so she had been called in to see me. My chest felt tight. I knew I had done the wrong thing. The shame of me admitting I felt I couldn't go on living was nothing compared to the shame I felt now. I was here where I shouldn't have been. I was an inconvenience and a problem. I didn't belong in this cubicle, I didn't belong anywhere.

I don't know how long she spent with me. Every moment was awkward and seemed to last forever. She spent most of her time looking down at her tick-box questionnaire. How was I doing, I wondered. What do those ticks mean? How many ticks do you get before you're carted off and sectioned or labelled as a psychopath? When she asked me what my plan was when I had said I didn't trust myself I didn't quite know what to say. "What exactly do you mean, Rebecca?" she questioned. "Have you taken anything, tried anything, got anything in mind?" No, I said. I hadn't taken anything. No, I hadn't tried anything. No, I didn't have anything set in my mind. All I knew was I couldn't see a way forward. I was desperately struggling to live through the despair I felt, the hopelessness and hatred I felt about myself and the feeling that I didn't warrant a place or belong on this earth was intensely strong. 'Hate' was too weak a word to describe how I viewed myself. I despised who I was, I couldn't cope with life anymore. What a weak, selfish and pathetic individual I had turned into. "I just don't trust myself," is all I could say.

You don't even have a suicide plan! Ha! This woman isn't going to take you seriously, you don't even mean it! What are you doing?!

What the hell were you thinking saying that?

She thinks you've just had a bad day at the office or something. TELL HER

She hasn't got time to be bothered with you!

Tell her how you really feel, Becki, tell her.

No, I can't find the words. There are no words.

Just no words.

I have always been grateful that thought bubbles don't appear over my head. I had not always been true to others about how I feel in everyday life. I don't think you can be if you're someone like I was, a people-pleaser. How can you be honest to others when you care more about what they think than you do about yourself? I have always liked that secret world of your own thoughts. No one needs to know anything about what you feel, only just what you say, and the feeling that thoughts can always be kept separate from the verbal and physical response if you become a master of pretence. We all do it, don't we? Think something but often say something different, sometimes nothing at all? But now I wished some narrator would pop up a speech bubble. I wished the words I couldn't articulate would be just written for me and appear for her to see so I didn't have to try to explain what I couldn't. For once in my life I wanted the true feelings to be seen. Cartoons featured in Private Eye. Taking the Mick out of a political story of the month. David gets it delivered and I often browse it over a morning coffee. What story is hidden this time behind humour, in pictures and a few chosen words above the characters' heads? I wished I was a cartoon. I wished she could possibly try to understand my story. My picture wasn't right, I was more than just upset. The old me was slowly dying, my mind had turned on me and was attacking me from the inside.

"Does your husband know you're here? Mm, well, how do you think he would feel about this? You have left him at home with two children and not told him how you feel? That is incredibly selfish, Rebecca. What help do you want? It seems to me you don't know what you want."

At this point, I looked at her and felt that last tiny strand of hope I had fade away. How could I have been so stupid? Why had I listened to myself? What the hell was I doing? She was right. David and the kids at home, totally unaware of this trip here. I felt so very bad, so guilty, and was riddled with shame. They had been at the centre of my thoughts all evening. I was here for them. I didn't want to die, deep down I wanted to live, I was dying to live. But this thing, this mist over me had pushed them away. I felt myself fading. The grasp I held over my mind was diminishing quickly. My logic of getting some help to try to save me, us, my family, was gone. *They would be better off without me.* That resonated through my every waking moment. This thing had taken over me, my thoughts were not my own, I was so detached from any love. They would be better off without me.

See, there is nothing wrong with you!

You should have told her. You should have said more Becki

You fool! Ha!

No words, I can't

You worthless, selfish person. Trying to help yourself? More like making an idiot of yourself!

You don't deserve that beautiful family at home!

Go and die! Get it over with!

I stuttered when I spoke. I was broken. I knew that even if no one could see it. I knew all the secrets in my world and that's where they should have stayed.

"I don't know what help I need, I just don't trust myself anymore."

That's all I could say over again. I wanted to say so much more but what did it matter now? I wanted to scream 'help me', 'save me', 'do something', but the words couldn't form verbally. I came to get help from professionals, yet they could not recognize what I needed. The woman had told me I didn't have any mental health problems, she couldn't understand what had brought me to this state. What was wrong? Where was the reasoning? A family crisis? A bereavement? Redundancy? What had happened? I couldn't even begin to explain, and she couldn't begin to see.

The only words I could manage were dismissed, the feelings I tried to explain and the thoughts of actions I was mentally trying to reason with were pointless. There was nothing that justified any help for me, sat in a busy A and E department taking a bed up that should have someone in need in, a victim of some awful accident, a tragedy that had unfolded on some poor citizen going about their everyday life, not me. Not a person who wanted to die because they didn't know how to live anymore and could not even articulate why.

Now, I have always been a soft person. Held my tongue far too much just to keep the peace. Character traits of a people-pleaser all over. But for a split-second, anger raged through me. It takes a lot of courage to ask for help and the last bit of strength I had was used up walking in here. I wanted to speak, to shout and to die right there and then. Yet all I could do was sob.

"I think a holiday would be good for you or a stay at your friends, a bit of a girly laugh. Coming into hospital isn't a holiday, is it? See your GP next week if you don't feel any brighter and she may see if you qualify for a counselling course but really there is nothing you need accept a good sleep. We all have bad days. You don't need to be on psychiatric ward, Rebecca, and you can't be given any tablets as you said you could do something silly. A good sleep and tomorrow you will wonder why you wasted your evening in here."

Bad day? You have no idea
You should have told her Becki
How? I can't say the words
Just say it, just say it
You've made a fool of yourself, she wouldn't understand, nobody will
Nobody can help you
You're a waste of space

I regretted being so honest with her immediately. If I could have grabbed the words spoken in that cubicle and swallowed them back into my mouth, I would have done. It didn't matter, nothing

I said mattered. I wanted to leave, to escape. I wasn't safe here. I wasn't safe anywhere. I never realized until that evening that saying you felt suicidal wasn't enough. I never knew you had to act on it to be taken seriously. Mental illness had to be seen like a physical one; saying how you felt wasn't enough. I never realized you had to prove your feelings to be heard.

This woman had misunderstood me, my outward image. There was no comprehension of the few words I could say. Face value, my years of mastering pretence were so ingrained that even though I wasn't consciously trying to show her I was OK, that was all she could see. A storm in a teacup. A hormonal woman overreacting, a woman who just needs to get a grip. My lack of explanation only symbolised a lack of a problem.

Sitting alone in the cubicle taking up space that I shouldn't have, I could barely breathe. What was I to do now? Go home and pretend this never happened? Pull myself together and get on with living? But it was too hard to live. I looked round the square space I had, cornered off only by floral-patterned curtains. Life went on, but how could mine? I could hear the faint murmur of conversations between staff members at the nurse's station, the phone ringing and the sound of a stretcher being pushed along the corridor. Outside of these curtains life indeed did go on. The buzzer on the wall, you know the one, press it for attention and a nurse will come to help you. I looked at that button. I had pressed the button when coming in this evening and those who came hadn't helped me. Walking through the doors of this place was my 'pressing of the button'. I wondered, if I had come in my pyjamas with no makeup on would things have been different? If my Prada jacket wasn't laid beside me on the bed, would people have seen I needed help then? Obviously, if I was fit enough to work there was nothing wrong with me, was there? A nurse interrupted my thoughts. She came in to tell me that they had phoned my husband, my next of kin, and that he was coming to collect me. I wasn't mortified or shocked. Normally I would have been. What would he say? But I simply did not care. I was past the point of no return, I had asked for help. I did what was directed at me. Google said to do it. It was the advice given to people on websites, on medication packets. But I was wrong. I was a time waster. I was stupid. After all, the assessor said, "If you really wanted to kill yourself you wouldn't be here, Rebecca."

Maybe she was right, this woman who had assessed me and cleared me of any mental illness. "Do you drink?" she asked me. "Maybe if you did it would help you," she laughed, "help you unwind a bit. Not in excess but a glass every evening always helps busy workers like us. We all have trying days and get overwhelmed every now and again, Rebecca." How petty I felt. I sat there waiting for David, feeling calm for the first time that day. There was a stillness about me. I had cried all I possibly could. I was out of everything. Out of feelings, out of emotions, out of living. I looked at the buzzer on the wall. It was mounted in a little case. I reached over for it and put it on my bed.

I closed my eyes and tried to pray. I tried to talk to God and ask for help. But I couldn't pray, I wasn't praying, I was choking on the words. Was this a punishment? I had tried to ask for help. A professional couldn't see I needed it. So I didn't need it, did I? What was wrong with me? Nothing but being a failure, I couldn't cope with life. There was no cure for me not coping. I was an idiot, a waste of space. I couldn't function, was incapable of thinking straight and I had neither hope nor will to live. I didn't know who I was or what had happened to my mind.

The girl I used to be
Has a terrible case of mistaken identity
Yesterday's girl is not what you see
It's a terrible case of mistaken identity

I looked to God for reasoning and understanding. Was I a bad person? Was this why I was trapped in some hell that no one could see? I couldn't pray. Why would he listen to me? Look at this worthless individual you've become, I told myself. Why would God help you? When there is nothing certain left to know, how the cracks begin to show.

God won't listen to you. Suicidal thoughts are a sin.

He gives life and he takes it. He will punish you now.

But I haven't done that, I haven't tried to kill myself. He may see I am struggling and help me.

He won't help you, why would he help you? You're a failure.

It would be better if you did die, you're a waste of space.

Look at you here taking up a bed and there is nothing wrong with you. Time waster.

If you needed help they would have helped you here! Pathetic!

And now Dave's on his way, what is he going to think of his weak wife?

What will the children think? You don't love them, you can't otherwise you wouldn't be here.

You're such a failure.

I picked up the buzzer and the calmness remained. It can be over within a few seconds, I thought. Pain-free in a few moments. That, or live like this. And the added shame of my husband now knowing what I had done: walked into a busy A and E department and told people I could no longer cope with life. I couldn't pretend to him now, could I? After all he had done for me. David always

24

coped. He took everything and no matter what life threw at him, he was a fighter. The shame that me, his wife, had done this, and for what? I would have to explain myself, and how could I do that when I have no words? I had lost control of life. This overwhelming pull towards peace was only given through the thought of dying. Grasping for control. What could I control? I could control if I lived or died. I could take charge of that. I couldn't control life, my thoughts, what happened anymore in any aspect of my existence, but I could control something. I found the cord wrapped around my neck and felt the plastic wire fall under my silk scarf. It felt cold against my skin and my hands slipped with sweat on the cord. I closed my eyes and thought about my three special people. I told God I loved them, begged him to let them know and asked him for forgiveness. My quest for peace had selfishly overseen anything else. I simply did not know how to live. I pulled the cord with both hands and immediately felt the tightness around my neck. Calmly I talked to myself, that's it, tighter tighter. It will be over within a minute. I began to feel lightheaded, dreamy, but the cord was slipping, the sweat from my hands lost grip and I couldn't hold the cord any tighter. It was then when I heard my husband's voice. He was always a larger than life character, his voice could always be heard before he was seen. He wasn't his bubbly self now, though. There was a tone in his voice, unnerved and shaken. I heard the nurse say she would find out which cubicle I was in.

I dropped the cord. I could barely see straight and the room was spinning. Was it David or was it a dream? The buzzer fell to my side and the tears came again, just like they did earlier in the evening. The curtains were opened and David walked in. He looked so worried, nervous and panic stricken. He didn't say anything, he just held me tightly and kept hold of me. I went to hold him back but something had changed. I loved him like I always had, but I wasn't there. We were disconnected, I couldn't feel him. I glanced down at the buzzer and felt numb. Many minutes passed before he pulled back and looked at me, tears running down his face. Not for the first time in my life, he had saved me.

Back at home, I got undressed in our en suite. I let my clothes just fall to the floor. Everything was the same as the previous morning: the same towel on the rail; my perfume bottle exactly where I had left it. Nothing had changed yet everything had. Looking in the mirror was a woman I hated. She wasn't me. She wasn't the person I knew. She was an unrecognizable failure in every way. I still had the remains of yesterday's makeup on, patchy, and I was a mess from all the crying, my face looked bloated and tired. As I undid my silk scarf, the marks from the cord were still visible on my neck. I ran my fingers over them. Did I actually do that? Was it a nightmare or did it really happen? David's bedside alarm began to ring. 6AM. He was downstairs brewing coffee. Since we got home he hadn't returned to bed. He was trying to make sense of why I had taken myself to A and E. Everything was going to be OK, perfect again right? He just couldn't understand what had gone so wrong that it made me walk in there. I was coping, surely I was? I always did.

I had been up a whole night and I was an unrecognizable person by the time a new day had dawned. Instead of getting ready for work and starting the day, I put on my dressing gown and sat on the side of my bed. David came up with a coffee and kissed my forehead. "Rest today," he said. "I will go into work and get the rest of the week off so we can be together." He looked exhausted and vulnerable and so very sad. His eyes looked heavy, he was tearful and so perplexed by what had happened. The sound of the children filled downstairs. The piano sprung into life with my son's regular morning practice of his repertoire. It was a new day. They were blissfully unaware of what had happened during the night. Life was how it had always been. I heard David tell them that I had a headache and wasn't going into work today. Little did they know about what had really happened to their mother. I silently wished them a good day and hoped they could hear me.

From the edge of my pillow, I saw my phone flash. I had silenced it, often wondered if you could silence the mind like you can a mobile phone. Mute it when you don't want to deal with people at that time, silence life, turn it off until you were ready. Wouldn't it be nice to 'turn off'? Just stop it all? It was a text from a friend. Five positives from her day. Something we often did this to celebrate the good things that were often overlooked by the general chaos of life. We agreed over a brew at Sainsbury's a while back that it was always good to focus on the positives no matter how small, and as good friends we would make sure we helped each other see these little important things.

Went for a run – feel invigorated!
New contract for APCs
George made breakfast! And it was delicious!
Stu got man of the match last night!
Treated myself to a new dress, gotta love online shopping over breakfast – bargain!
Text me yours??

I had more than five negatives but not one single positive. Simply no words. I put the phone back under my pillow, for there was no reply to be sent. As the day began for everyone but me, I knew life would never be the same again. That moment, at that time, I didn't know how to live, how to feel or even how to be. I knew nothing. I wasn't fearful, I wasn't calm. Just empty. I told myself, sleep now. If the pain doesn't ease, you can always die tomorrow.

Life could wait.

> *"I can't explain myself, I'm afraid, Sir,*
> *because I'm not myself you see"*

Alice in Wonderland

DISCONNECTED

Who am I, what am I, how did I get here?

I woke up to the sound of the bins getting dragged across the road and the clatter of the plastics being tipped into the waste removal truck. The hiss of the engine of the rubbish crusher and the muffled conversation between the workers. It was collection day. I cannot tell you last time I was home for collection of the bins. Not that it is important, is it. No one has it on the calendar, I don't think? We just know the routine of which coloured bin and which week if we are lucky enough to remember the day. If not, seeing the neighbours' ones out is usually a prompt reminder for us all. Many a time I have dashed out to the car running late in the morning to glance over the road and curse the bins. Forgotten again. Quick mad dash back up the drive, wheel them down, then on my way.

I leaned up and peaked below the blind. I don't think I've seen the bin men in a long time. Funny to think that life goes on in so many ways whilst we are living. I mean, logically, of course, the bins were emptied. I generally was the one who dragged them back up the drive, so I knew they had been, but I never thought about it. Never once thought about the fact that life goes on and we are not a part of it, whether it be about the bins or anything else.

It was a dull, damp day. After the rain and wind that came yesterday it was a surprise to see the stillness from my window despite the overcast. The grey clouds covered the sky and the surface water from the storm made the tarmac shine, but the trees waved calmly in a gentler breeze than what I remembered from the previous day. Maybe the calm before another storm. The chap who returned my bins didn't look that cold. No hat on and his fluorescent jacket was left open. Maybe he was hot from the rushing back and forth from the truck. I saw a small bird fly towards the feeding stand at the front of the garden. How peaceful would it be to be that little sparrow? Just following its instinct. No time to arrive and no time to leave. Just time to soar and time to fly free. Such a small, fragile creature that was free and able to survive on its own. I wished I was that little bird. It seemed so carefree.

What time was it? This new world I was in, home throughout the day, it felt uncomfortable. I was incredibly tired. 11.34am. I rolled back over and pulled the duvet up higher. The truck hissed again as it moved on down the lane, and as it did I lay in bed trapped and frozen in this unknown reality which I was unable to drive away from. The morning after. Wow, with each waking moment reality came clearer and clearer to me. *What on earth have you done? My goodness, you should be at work, what are you playing at? Did that all even happen?* Oh, it did. I knew it had. My gut told me so. I felt sick. Physically sick. I brought my legs up towards my chest and hugged my knees to my body trying to make myself feel warmer. *Breathe, Becki, stop shaking, calm down.* My mind raced, snippets of flashbacks from the past 24 hours appeared before my eyes. Blurred moments were recalled to my mind. That woman, the buzzer, the noise of the department, the smell of the clinical detergent in the ladies, the poster signs on the wall. It had happened. It was real. I bolted. Straight to the bathroom. Threw my head over the toilet whilst kneeling on the cold wooden floor where this unstoppable sickness came over me.

The house was so quiet. I hadn't ever known it to be quiet so still. No noise from the dogs either. David must have put them out in the kennels before leaving this morning. Standing in the kitchen pouring a glass of water, I felt dizzy and weak. When was the last time I had eaten? I wasn't hungry at all. My stomach churned but it wasn't for food. I sat down on the breakfast stool. *Take sips of water, Becki, little sips.* My hand shook when it held the glass. The coldness of the chilled water made my grasp questionable, just like my hold of reality, the glass seemed to slip from my hold when I tried to pick it up. *Use two hands, hold it properly.* I looked around the kitchen. Breakfast pots left on the side by the sink, David's 'Private Eye' on the sideboard and the signed trip letter which should had gone with my daughter back to school left on the breakfast bar. Signs of an everyday normal life. A normal family kitchen in a normal family home.

The large family picture caught my eye. All four of us. Must be about five, maybe six years ago now. Four laughing faces. I remember that day so clearly. We had booked a ferry to Ireland. A cottage on the coast just south of Cork. Us, two kids and two dogs. We sat on the ferry all excited. Off to explore new ground together, unknown possibilities and relaxing times lay ahead. An escape from daily life for seven wonderful days with no work, no school, no commitments and no distractions. I set the timer on my phone camera and propped it against the window then dashed back and leaned in next to David. It captured a beautiful moment. What was felt inside was shown outside. I felt peaceful, happy and so contented with life. We got it made into a painted canvas. It made us all smile. It was special, what it captured was special. The trip was memorable for many reasons and that picture captured the family's spirit, unity, and sense of freedom we had in the world together.

I walked over to the canvas. I studied our faces, trying to remember feeling at ease like I knew I was then. The person in that photo wasn't me now. Somehow, somewhere, between that photo and today, that person had got lost. This new person was a stranger. She did not fit into any photos like that, any family like that. She did not even fit into her own skin. It was unknown what it was like to feel peace or a sense of belonging that picture portrayed. The word was a concept she couldn't understand. I longed to go back to that boat, to that time and to that moment. The dizziness came over me again and so did the tears. I stepped back towards the stool but my eyes stayed focused on that picture. We all have our own picture, our own reality. The paint looked firm from a distance, but close up on the image of me, the paint seemed to be running, slowly dripping, the colours merging, mixed and undefined. The canvas underneath was cracking, the foundations were broken. The colour only holds for so long when the foundations are crumbling underneath. My world was crumbling and, in the process, I was breaking apart everyone else's as well.

I had never felt that magnetic pull back to my bed like I had done that day. Fear overcame me. The crumbling picture before my eyes scared me. I wasn't safe. Not in my own kitchen, not in my own home, not in my own mind. I was not safe at all. The kitchen seemed so exposed all of a sudden. I heard rain falling on

the conservatory roof, the extension that led on from the breakfast bar, all those windows – the outside world right there. A sheltered garden that was hardly overlooked, but still, open. There was an eeriness that took over. Grey skies had darkened the light from the windows and brought a fearful panic to me.

I had to get to my bed. I had to escape. Heading back upstairs, I realized how open I was. The blind at the bottom of the stairs has been pulled up. I hadn't noticed it on my way down. I could see across the lane, anyone could see me. I was exposed. There in my dressing gown, I was unsafe, vulnerable and unprotected. The rain was falling heavier now, the bouncing on the conservatory roof increased to a more thunderous noise and the shrubs in the front garden were blowing back and forth by the window. I raced upstairs, the felt presence of something there behind me, with me, surrounding me. I had to get to my bed, I had to hide.

I pulled the covers over and sunk down into a haven of isolation, unseen and hidden. Tissues scattered from when I had come to bed earlier. I hadn't known I had cried myself to sleep. *It's OK now. Calm down. Stay here for a while longer and then think about what you are going to do.* What was I going to do? What day was it again? I had no sense of time. My phone. I reached for my phone under my pillow. Still on silent. 10 messages, four missed calls, three voicemails, six WhatsApp messages and 15 Facebook notifications. Work. I was supposed to be at work. Once I realized this, there was no sudden panic, no 'think on your feet' response, no nothing. I simply did not care. I did not care if they thought I was dead or alive, if they had to cancel the whole clinic of patients, if I faced disciplinary action. I felt nothing. I couldn't even feel sorry. Letting people down has never been something I ever did. Do more rather than less, be more rather than less. But today I did not care. I had lost the ability to feel, to think. There was no sense of guilt for my work colleagues, for the patients. I didn't feel anything. Maybe David informed them. No, no he wouldn't have. He never knew where I was working. It changed frequently and he would have never known where I was to be based and who I was working with today. Wakefield, Manchester, Birmingham. Where was I even meant to be? I looked at the list of notifications on my phone. Yes, work, wondering where I was. I called the voicemail. One message from my line manager, she sounded stern, cross and reminding me I was in. The second a little less stern and the third sounded more of a concerned tone. "Please ring me, Rebecca, when you get this message." What was I to say? I had no words to say anything. What was wrong? Call in and say what? How on earth could I explain not turning up and not even calling in? How could I put into any verbal conversation that I could not possibly leave my bed, never mind my house? And for what reason? It didn't matter anyway. I wasn't worried, concerned nor bothered. The reality of it had sunk in. I knew what I had done but what I was doing, the implications, the situation I was creating, I couldn't care. It was impossible for me to feel anything. There was no penny dropping moment of, "Oh shit, Becki." Simply the will to close my eyes and not face anything. Nothing at all.

You're not safe.

Look at you. An adult. Hiding, in bed. Under a duvet.

You've let all those people down. What will they think of you now?

What on earth are you doing?

You've most likely lost a good job and for what??

Why are you behaving like this?

Nutter.

Close your eyes and just die.

You are not safe. Not here. Not anywhere.

Sleep, Becki, just get some sleep.

Sleep. I just wanted to sleep. To leave this world and to escape. I touched the text message icon. David.

Hope you've managed a sleep and feel better. I'm off for the next two days, we can do something nice. Don't forget to get the kids from school, set the alarm and have a rest today. Love you darling xx

The kids. I would have to get the kids. *No, I can't leave the house. No. I won't. David will get them, he must. What time is it?* Panic overcame me. How could I go out, out there and collect the children? I could have to drive, to see people, No. I couldn't. It was only lunch time. *Becki, calm down. Another four hours before the kids finish school. Four hours. Get some more sleep.* I opened the text from David. I went to text him back. There were no words to type. I didn't have the words to say. I reread his message. 'Set your alarm.' So, that's what I did. Alarm set for 3.45pm.

Drifting in and out of conscious thought, the afternoon soon passed. It was a whirlwind of travel into the depths of some very dark places, snapped back to reality every now and again with sharp chest pains, shallow breathing and sweats of terror. Swirling thoughts and visions swept across my mind. Work, the family, the future. I could see my manager angrily marching around on the phone cancelling clinics, theatres not prepared, patients not prepped. I could see David explaining to his boss why he needed time of suddenly and having to explain the circumstances, as otherwise he wouldn't be granted leave. I could see situations that I was involved in and I felt the fear they produced. How could I face people again? I felt an intense fear of living yet an emptiness at the same time. These thoughts were my own yet I did not belong in them nor the version of reality I was seeing. A fear of taking back the covers and being present in this world, a world I know longer had any sense of belonging in.

3.45pm. Off went the alarm.

Becki, you must get the kids.

You're not even dressed.

GET UP AND GET THE KIDS.

If I was dead, someone else would have to get the kids.

Someone else could sort life out.

You're a selfish sod, those kids deserve better.

The kids – what will I say to the kids? I want to stay in bed.

I don't want to see the kids; I can't see the kids.

Go and pick them up then come back to bed. Say you have a headache.

You're a pathetic mother.

I got up. How was I going to do this? I had to drive eight miles in a round trip, to the school and back. It seemed like a challenge as big as climbing Everest. I had to leave the house. What if I saw someone? I had to drive, be alert and be present. Yet I knew I was not at all. The clothes I had worn at the weekend working the dogs were on the sideboard. I kept them back from the wash as they weren't dirty as such, just slightly muddy around the ankles of the joggers. They will do, I thought. Put them on. I avoided the mirror. There was no need to look at myself. That wasn't me. That image I imagined wasn't who I was, an imposter had taken over. The reflection any mirror would give me would only show a stranger trapped in my body. Forcing one step in front of the other, I headed back downstairs to the kitchen. I avoided looking at the open window in the hallway, and the family portrait. Straight to the back door to put on my old trainers. I knew I had to do this. I had to get the children. I was not so far gone as to have lost my complete sense of reality, but I was merely hanging on by a thread.

Don't think about, it just do it.

Pull yourself together, Becki.

What if I see someone? What if they talk to me?

You won't, just go.

If I was dead, I wouldn't have to do this.

Look at you, dressed like this. What a mess you look.

Opening the front door. It sounds so easy, doesn't it? Put in a key, turn the lock, lift the handle and there you go. I had never had any problems before like this. But something had changed. This door was more than just an entrance or an exit. This door was a protector. It kept me safe from the outside world. Behind it I could hide, out there I was exposed and naked. Unsafe. Pain pounded through my chest. My heartbeat was so very strong that

I could feel it against my ribs, and a stabbing-like pain took my breath way. My hands were shaking as I touched the handle. The tears came and my surroundings were blurred. The sensation of spinning came over me and I lowered myself against the wall to sit down on the tiled entrance hall.

What were my options? I had to talk to myself rationally. *Come on, Becki, think.* What could I do? I could phone David. And say what? I could phone a friend or text them – I could text them? No need to speak at all that way. But then, if they did collect the kids I would have to see them when they dropped the kids off at home and invite them in… NO. That would be even worse. There is only one option. *Pull yourself together, you can be back in 15 minutes.* It was then I suddenly realized that any interaction with anyone was just as frightening as going out. 15 minutes. I looked at my watch. *OK, 15 minutes.*

That was it. With an intense headache, chest pain and shivering limbs I got back up on my feet, legs so weak I thought they might give way. I opened the door and looked at my car. *Go. Go, Becki.* That moment was an unconscious thought that little did I know would form the behaviour of my mindset for the foreseeable future. I got in the car and autopilot took over. The radio came on, and without really knowing how, I found myself at the roundabout where I was turning off to meet the children down by the back of the field. There was no sense of time, just a heightened sense of reality that took over me. Shadows from the hedges became darker, dangerous. I was edgy, nervous, exposed and afraid of what not so long ago I loved. The fields, the narrow country roads, they seemed scary open places as I drove towards the town. The whole area was so vast with trees that could be hiding hidden dangers to shock me at any time.

Did I stop at the traffic lights? I didn't even remember seeing any lights, yet I must have gone through four sets. How I had physically driven there was beyond my understanding. It must have been simply a physical function as I was not there in mind and barely in body. I thought back to a night out I had been on years ago, I must have been 18, 19 maybe. That night I had to walk home after running out of money for a taxi so I got out of the cab at my friends and walked the rest of the way. I *was* sensible, I knew it was stupid, yet I did it anyway. I took my heels off and walked on the road. Not in a drunken way, simply because it was brighter from the street lights on the road than on the pavement. The darkness of walls and the shadows from gates. Anyone could be hiding behind them. So, I walked barefoot in the road home. It was only a 10-minute walk. The adrenaline kicked in. I was in a state of alert, scanning for danger, checking behind me, fast footsteps wondering what, who was hidden behind every dark shadow. That flight or fight response. I was ready, not entirely sure what for, but I was ready. A fear, danger, a heartbeat that was so fast I felt it coming though my chest. That was the last time I had felt quite like this. This 'high alert'. Yet there was a potential danger then; there was none present now.

The children swung the car doors open. Sports kits were thrown in the boot and two lively teenagers got into the car. Laughing and joking between them, they were carefree and oblivious to the different worlds we were now living in. I certainly wasn't here, with them. I heard them talking, I heard them telling me about their days yet nothing registered. *Home. Go home.* The car was driving itself I am sure. Head pounding and my chest tight, I simply repeated myself again and again. *Home.* I couldn't bear to attempt any conversation. The mother who wanted to know about her children's days at school wasn't the person driving that car. The mother who instantly smiled when she saw the most precious things to her wasn't here. It was a terrible case of mistaken identity.

What am I?

Where am I?

How did I get here?

"How's your day been, Mum? Has your headache gone?"

"Mum?"

Funny how you hear the words but they can't form on your tongue. I had never experienced this before. I could not communicate with my own children. I could see my eldest trying to catch my attention in the wing mirror.

Hellfire, Becki, pull yourself together

You're not safe out here

Home. I just need to be home

Answer the kids

If I was dead, I wouldn't have to face this.

This is pathetic, what the hell is wrong with you?

What a waste of space. You should have killed yourself yesterday

Just say you have a headache still

There is danger, you are not safe.

Get home

"Not the best, I still have a really bad head."

I spoke quietly and my voice was shaky. I wanted the world to stop. I wanted to be the person I was 48 hours ago, not this, this stranger whom I did not recognize. I wanted to be hidden away, to be alone. Whatever the children said back to me did not register. As I pulled up outside the house, the rush of wanting to get through the door to the other side engulfed me. I told the children to quickly get their things and not mess about. I needed to be home. I needed to be hidden and I needed to be safe. The sense of panic did not stop even when I stepped inside. I spoke briefly to the children without looking at them, I could not make eye contact. Fruit, showers, homework, Dad will sort dinner, bad head, need sleep. Just a spiel of words given as I focused on the stairs. *Get back to your room, Becki.* That was the first time I had not greeted the children with a hug, an excited and pleased-to-see-them welcome. The first time I did not get them a drink and a piece of fruit whilst they got changed. The first time I did not care.

Getting back into bed, I realized how much pain I was in. My head was pounding which matched my heartbeat. I was sweating so much yet freezing cold. I got under the duvet and wrapped the fleece overthrow around me keeping my clothes on. *Home. Back here hidden.* I had not realized I had been crying until I felt the wetness on the pillow against my cheek.

It's OK, you're home now
Fancy leaving the kids downstairs like that
What kind of a mother are you?
Sleep, Becki
You pathetic sod

My mind began to race, my stomach began to turn over. The feel of the fleece blanket was reassuring, wrapped round tight I made sure every inch of me was covered. I made myself as small as possible, covered under a protective layer, just a little gap above my head so I could breathe. *Close your eyes, calm down, you're back safe now.* The subconscious state of turmoil took over me. Not sleep, yet not reality. Flashes of visions before my eyes, a journey that gave me moments of calm and then moments of utter fear. Real fear. Before I knew it, the throw was kicked off. I was trapped, panicking and hysterical. I had to get out, I had to escape and find somewhere safe. Sweating in a panic I rose to my feet and headed into the en suite. So hot, yet freezing cold I scooped up some running tap water and drank from my hand. Sitting down on the closed toilet seat I could hear the children downstairs practising their music, the sound of a tractor chugging past and birds singing in the trees outside the house. Why was life happening to everyone else but me? Feeling physically weak I slowly headed back to the bed. Every step was guilt ridden. My children were downstairs, doing their practice, and I would not bear to be with them or a part their life. I had travelled so far on a journey in my mind, disconnecting from life. I wanted the music to silence. I wanted everything to stop. I made my shelter, back in my bed, my block aid to the world once again, and took some deep breaths. Incredibly tired. I was so very tired. It was when I was lying in bed, dipping in and out of slumber I heard the front door open and the faint chatter of conversation. It was David, he was home. I realized the front door, the barrier between me and that world out there was not ever going to protect me. Because it was me I was unsafe from. What had happened had destroyed my thinking. I could not escape my own mind, my own thoughts and this reality. It was me that I feared now.

God knows, sometimes I just don't understand.
Wouldn't it be easy to just turn the page?
Wouldn't it be better to throw the book away?
How do you love when you're broken?
I've had enough.
I'm only human.

The days that followed are a blur of existence. David did indeed take a few days off work. Looking back now, his presence, ironically, helped me disconnect from the world. I could rest, I stayed in bed. Of course, that's what I needed, wasn't it? Just a few days' rest and I would be back to it and all this would fade away. Back to handling life again. I was just overtired, wasn't I? My responsibilities, unspoken yet handed over to David so as the pressure to exist in the normal world I had once known eased, I drifted further into isolation, into a disorientated state. Hours merged and turned into days. Conscious moments of extreme fear to jaded moments of disorientation, not knowing where I was. Whatever happened to me over those days, life went on. For all those around me, life carried on regardless. I realized that life was going on despite my reluctance to engage in the hand I had been dealt. My phone still flashed with notifications. I turned it off. The landline still rang and brought me back to reality in a state of panic. I ignored it. David tried to converse with me. I just wanted to sleep, didn't respond to him.

I had forgotten what it felt like to be hungry. In fact, I could not remember the last time I ate something. Dave brought glasses of fresh juice up and side plates of my favourite biscuits to tempt me. He brought up bacon and eggs, soup, freshly made sandwiches cut into love heart shapes with a little notes. He tried everything, yet I was despondent and numb. I felt nothing. No emotions, no love. Only fear and panic if I got up from under the duvet. I had no desire to do anything, see anyone, speak to anyone or live. The only thing I wanted was to be set free from this cage that had suddenly engulfed me. The only way I could do that was to hide under the blanket and live in a semi-conscious world. The moments I faced in the real world were too difficult and the thought of escaping by dying was my only reoccurring thought every moment, and the only thing that brought me any slight comfort.

David had taken over sorting the children out. I wasn't sure how they were, or how he was. How had school been? I hadn't seen them at all. I didn't know if Dave had remembered to give them their vitamins or checked their school homework planners. What alarmed me most was how I did not care anymore, and that wasn't me. Detached and emotionless, all I could think was that when I die, life will go on, all this will go on, it goes on now without me, it will do then. Mentally redundant, unneeded and pointless to existence.

"Becki, we need to talk."

David sat down on the bed. His tone was firm, he sounded tired.

"You need to see a doctor, Becki. I want to take you this afternoon to the surgery."

I didn't want to talk to him. I didn't want to see him. I wanted to stay hidden. *Say something, Becki. Say something.*

"Becki, you need to come out from under the duvet and talk to me."

He was getting impatient. I sensed his frustration. He pulled back the blanket.

"NO!"

"Don't do that. Give it me back."

I snatched the covers back. I did not want to be exposed like this. He had opened the curtains and daylight filled the room. The panic swelled inside of me. David, he looked tired. I had not seen him properly since that night at the hospital. He has been around of course, but I hadn't seen him to look at, I just sensed his presence and heard his voice. He looked angry and sad. Part of me wanted to reach out to him, I loved this man so very much. I wanted to hold him and feel part of us again. But I couldn't. I could not do that. I had left him behind. I had shut down.

"You need to see a doctor. You have been in bed for days, you won't get up, you won't eat, you won't see anyone. We need to get

44

you some help, you've got to see someone, go on some tablets or something."

I tucked the blanket around me and felt the softness against my skin. David went to stroke my face but I moved away without even thinking.

"How can I help you if you don't talk to me?"

He was cross now.

Where to begin?

No words to say how it is. No words.

"I don't want to live anymore."

Tears began to fall. I felt so weak, so trapped and lost for words to try to explain anything. I didn't know what to say. I longed to hold him, I longed to feel his touch, but I couldn't. His eyes started to water. Glazed over with tears, his blue eyes shone in the sunlight from the window.

"I love you, Becki. I want my wife back. Let me help you."

I reached for his hand. I remember the feel of his skin and his eyes looked into mine. He told me he would keep me safe with him. He didn't realize I was physically only here. Mentally I was miles away. And it was me he needed to keep me safe from. Instinctively he got under the covers. He wrapped the blanket around us both and made my little cave once again. He held me whilst I cried myself to sleep.

When I woke up he was gone. I heard the radio on downstairs. I needed the bathroom, and painkillers. A banging headache thumped across my brow. Toilet first, then downstairs to the kitchen cupboard and back to bed. *I would do that. I can do it. 5 minutes max, that's all it will take.* I pulled down the blind and blocked out the world. I grabbed my dressing down and avoided catching my eye in the mirror in the en suite. *Now get the tablets and come straight back upstairs. You can do that.* Heading downstairs I felt shaky. Washing was in little colour-coordinated piles at the top of the stairs. The house smelt fresh and the banister shone in the sunlight. Biscuit was sat in his usual place, right at the bottom of the stairs; I had forgotten about Biscuit and Poppy. His whole body rushed with excitement when he saw me. His tail banging against the bottom step, his body back and forth not knowing quite what to do with himself. Then the barking as he launched his way up the stairs to greet me. Biscuit wasn't allowed upstairs. He knew that. He circled me on the stairwell and nearly knocked me over. Round and round. *Go away, Biscuit.* I could not be bothered with him. I held onto the rail for support. Feeling weak I longed to be back upstairs under the blanket in the dark.

"He's pleased to see you."

"Down, boy. Biscuit get down now"

David looked up and smiled. He looked focused, busy. Better than earlier. He looked determined.

"Come and sit in the conservatory. It's a beautiful afternoon. I will get you a drink."

His tone wasn't asking; he was telling me. *No, just need a tablet then back to bed, Becki. Tell him. Back to bed.* Summoning the words to speak was harder than doing what I was instructed. He had been ironing. The back doors were open and piles of neatly ironed clothes were stacked up on the breakfast bar. The sound of the water fountain and the birds singing filled the room. I turned off the radio, my head banging with the noise. It was so bright, the sunlight. I sat down on the sofa and brought my knees up to my chest, my hands covering my eyes from the sun. David brought me some juice. He put it down on the glass table and lowered the blinds.

"It's great to see you downstairs, Becki. Biscuit has missed you. We have all missed you."

"I need some pain killers. I just need some tablets, that is all."

Without saying anything he got up and headed back into the kitchen. *What day was it? What time was it?* I felt nervous and unsafe. The doors were wide open. Outside was right there. Two tablets appeared in front of me. *If only these would stop the real pain. Stopped life.*

"I've put the water on so it will be nice a hot. A bath or a shower. What would you like?

Neither. I don't want any. I need to be back in bed.

"A freshen up will make you feel brighter, and whilst you're having a wash I will change the bed. Fresh clean sheets."

No, my bed is just fine, it is all just fine, just leave it alone.

I had no energy to speak. I had no ability to move the word that spoke in my mind out through my mouth.

It's been 15 minutes, you must get back upstairs. Becki, go back upstairs.

You can't even have a conversation!

Pathetic.

Tired. Am so tired.

Tired!! You lazy sod! What have you done?! Nothing. Yet you're tired?!!

I tried to focus my breathing. *Sip the juice and swallow these pills.* A bird landed on the edge of the water fountain. Nervously it looked around, in all directions, assessing danger. Was it safe? Could it stop there for a moment? It edged into the pool under the foundation and splashed around, quickly, momentarily before checking its surroundings yet again. A quick moment of bathing then back on high alert. Could anyone really be free? That bird could fly anywhere. There was no cage, no restrictions, yet it was so cautious, so fragile. It was on edge, waiting for danger, assessing risk. Where would it come from, what would it be? An unspeakable cautiousness that a little bird showed. Nothing was safe. I wasn't safe.

He had been talking to me.

"That's all, OK?"

I hadn't heard a word of what he was saying. My mind was elsewhere. The bird. The time, I should be back upstairs. He smiled and I nodded. He was taking charge. He had plans. I had no clue what these were, but I was under instruction. He took me by the hand. Before I knew it, a bath was running with Lush bath bombs fizzing away and bubbles from the Sanctuary Spa bubble bath coming up over the hand rail. The bed was stripped and fresh towels were laid out. I heard his voice but I did not comprehend what he was saying. Instructions, I heard instructions. "You can get in now, Becki". I did what I was told. I had lost the ability to think for myself. As my body sank below the water, and I felt covered and hidden by the bubbles, I wondered what it would be like to sink further. There was something relaxing about the water, the calmness of the movements, its stillness. I lowered my head, water filled my ears. Out on the landing, Dave was still talking, his voice now muffled. The stillness pulled me lower. My breathing was short but I was not panicked. I was drawn to the world beneath the water, where it was still and peaceful. The water rose further, I felt it enter my nostrils and I felt the back of my head touch the curve of the bath. *Just go. Just go, Becki.* I closed my eyes and let the water cover me. I felt a shadow over the water, the warm sun reflection from the window was blocked and a coldness came over. Dave's presence pulled me back into his world.

"Don't fall asleep in there!"

"Right, got you out some jeans and a top. We've got to go in 20 minutes."

Go where?

To get the kids?

He can get the kids.

I can't go out.

"I don't want to go out. I am tired. Just need to go back to bed now."

"Well you can after you've seen the doctor, remember – you agreed to see her so I have got us an appointment at half past. Won't take long and you will probably get some pills to make you feel better."

He was telling me how it was. There was no option, no choice. It was a direction. *I don't remember agreeing to this.* I didn't even remember discussing it. Panic crept over me. Pain resonated throughout my chest, like all my ribs were sealing up and the weight of the water was crushing my whole body. The water suddenly went very cold and I felt exposed. I pulled myself up but my body was stiff, it hurt to move and spasms of pain shot down my spine and into my legs. He sensed the change in me. I wanted to get up, get out. I heard him talking but it made no sense. The panic was too much. I would have to leave the house. All I desperately wanted to do was to be back in bed hidden and safe. Not go out, not see people and not engage in anything. I had no energy for this, no energy for life.

Do what David says.

You're pathetic.

Just let me sleep, please stop, let me sleep.

I wouldn't have to do this if I was dead.

Go with him then come back. 15 minutes?

He will be with you, you don't need to say anything.
Die, Becki, just die.

"Will you make the bed again for me?"

"Once were back home, yes I will make the bed"

Getting to the doctor's surgery was a blur. It wasn't like the last time I went out, where everything seemed sharper, vivid and real. It was an out-of-body experience. Nothing registered. The pain in my chest intensified. My whole body pained. The headache had not gone from earlier, it had got worse and the movement of every limb painfully ached. David had put some clothes on the bed. He had helped me dress and talked to me the whole time, yet he was doing a good job of a two-way conversation all by himself. *Focus on your breathing, Becki.* The pain in my chest was so strong. Maybe I was having a heart attack? Maybe there was something else physically wrong with me that I was not aware of? Maybe the doctor would see this? Maybe it wasn't all in my head? If I breathed shorter breaths the pain wasn't quite as deep, so I focused on my breathing. I felt every breath and concentrated hard, *there, breathe like this, it is not as painful.* Distracted and totally disorientated, I found myself at the surgery having no knowledge or recollection of getting there.

I sat in the chair next to the table. It was an old room. Not a new clinical room with white-washed walls. A wooden desk, framed pictures of children next to the desktop. Posters up on the walls, muscular skeleton images and a heart labelled with zoomed-in close-ups of valves. David sat next to me and talked to the doctor. His tone seemed positive, hand gestures every now and again. She nodded on occasions. I didn't hear any of what they were saying. *Get home, Becki. Time to be back home now.* Where was the way out? Where was the door? *Behind David, the door is behind David.*

Just hang on another minute, we will be finished soon, just be patient. I sat on the edge of the chair ready to go, I was ready to go. It was hot, there was no air. My chest was tight and I was sweating. The examination bed caught my eye. Covered in that blue disposable roll, a little step up to it on the floor. There was a small box of toys on the bed to keep any restless children amused whilst they got checked over. I remembered being a child and being allowed to pick a toy to play with whilst I was sat on a similar bed. Why I was there I don't recall, but I remember my mum sat talking whilst I was in my vest and knickers on a bed like that with an old worn teddy as my companion. The doctor gave us both a sticker that day, one for me and one for Bear. I was proud. I was strong for Bear. I didn't cry when I had the needles as it wouldn't have been fair on him, he needed to see I didn't cry so he wouldn't cry. *Always got to be strong, Becki.*

"Rebecca, how are you feeling today?"

My guard went up. Words that formed in my mind were not coming down into my mouth. *I don't want to be here. I want to go home.*

"OK."

"Your husband tells me you haven't been yourself recently. Can you tell me how you've been feeling?"

"Tired."

"Do you want to tell me Rebecca what has happened? Your husband says you went to the hospital last week?"

Last week? What day is it now? Which hospital appointment? Did she know? What did that screen in front of her tell her? Will she know the updates from the private hospital? No, not an appointment, that visit... that was the other night. Must be that. Stay silent, Becki. Stay silent. I didn't want to talk about that. I did not want to think about it. Ever again. Visions of that night came flooding back. That woman, the place, the cord. Those words. I felt angry. The memory of that night – no. I would not talk about it. Nightmares of that night were so intense they partially blocked out the reason I had walked into A and E in the first place. I couldn't discuss any of it, that evening, that night, what happened, what I heard. No.

Remember what that woman said to you, Becki.

There's nothing wrong with you.

Time waster.

Useless waste of space.

You should have killed yourself then.

Saved wasting this doctor's time now.

"No. There is nothing wrong with me. I am just tired."

"There is a form here I would like you to look at, Rebecca. If you can answer the questions 1 to 10, 10 being the stronger feeling."

I looked down at this form. A printed piece of paper just typed up on Word. I heard David taking over the conversation, not eating, just sleeping, not doing anything. My mind raced with blurred memories of that evening. How can it be over a week ago? *There is nothing wrong with me. That woman said there was nothing wrong with me. It doesn't matter how I feel, if there isn't any physical evidence to prove it, it doesn't exist. Saying it means nothing. "You wouldn't be here if you wanted to die, Rebecca."* I felt guarded. I had to protect myself. I had asked for help. I had gone to get help. I wasn't in need of any. I just needed to cope again.

It was all in my mind, whatever was happening was in my mind. A failure on my part to handle life. If I could control my thoughts a bit, just a bit more sleep, that's all I need. There was nothing the matter with me. I was a fraud. It was invisible to everyone, if I meant what I had said I would have done it. I picked up the pen.

I didn't look at the questions, I just saw the numbers. *Circle the numbers and you can go home.* I circled the numbers, 1. All the way down. A word caught my eye. Suicidal thoughts. My mind raced. If I circled 10 what would that mean? No more than circling 1. No one could help me. I am the problem; my mind, my body is the problem. Trying to explain what I couldn't understand myself was not going to help me. I knew. I had tried. Without knowing it, I had lost trust in people. Something invisible had happened to me and went unseen. I heard the words I had said back at the hospital, however many nights past it was now, and they were pointless without evidence to back them up.

No one could see anything wrong with me, so there mustn't be. It was all in my head and I realized that when I walked of out that A and E department that night. I had left my trust in people there and brought home an even deeper-rooted self-hatred for who I was.

The doctor glanced down the score sheet. I felt her look at me but avoided eye contact. I caught the end of the conversation: no tablets... not needed... sleeping fine... just let her rest... give it another week... if things don't improve come back to see me... sick note for a week... just see how things go... rest and relaxation... lunch out... dog walks.... fresh air...

Home.
Get back home now.
See, Becki, you can do it.
You are OK.
You don't need any help.
Nothing can help you now anyway.
You can just die if you can't handle it.
Die if you can't handle it...

David wasn't happy, I could tell. He wanted a prescription. Some tablets that would kick in over the next 24 hours. He wanted an answer, a reason and a solution. He wanted his wife back and not this ridiculous excuse for a woman that I had turned into. Physically tired from my thoughts alone, I didn't notice any of the journey back. The pain was still there but duller, more like an aching body after a mountain hike the day before, it became background noise to my thoughts. *Home, safe at home hidden. Hidden, need to be hidden.*

"Will you make the bed now for me please?"

"Yes."

I had disconnected from the world I lived in. From everyone around me. And from who I was.

"We are all just a car crash, a diagnosis, an unexpected phone call, a newfound love or a broken heart away from becoming a completely different person. How beautifully fragile are we that so many things can take but a moment to alter who we are forever?"

Samuel Decker Thompson

FRAGILE

The days that followed turned into weeks without me knowing. I functioned on a merely physical level, which was somewhat questionable. More of a basic existence, 'functioned' gives more of the illusion that I was willingly taking part in things. I wasn't. I did the bare minimum I could and it took every ounce of effort I had. David returned to work. His presence at home in the days after my appearance at the hospital made my existence easier to disconnect from life I had once known, and his absence forced me back into that world. Every day waking up was filled with dread. David dropped the kids at school, I had to pick them up. The 4pm scenario came around fast. Housework, walking the dogs, ironing? Hell no. That was beyond comprehension. Breathe, hide, control the thoughts of wanting to die – they were my daily tasks and, believe me, every minute lasted hours.

I had no grasp on any sense of reality and it became apparent that the only control I had was over time. It became of great importance to me. I could control my mind if I could control the time I had to be unsafe for. Hidden, I could manage. I could cope with existing in that world, my mind would reassure me *I can always die tomorrow* when panic took over, but reality was a step into an illusion in which my thoughts were not my own, and I couldn't live with that, so I had to limit the time I was unhidden for. What I did not realize was that 'high alert' physical and mental adrenaline was a rush to protect you from a sudden impending potential danger. The feeling I had walking home in the early hours alone that morning many years ago, that feeling I had stepping out of my front door to go and collect the children. That high alert had become a state of mind, daily, every minute. Yet that adrenaline state was only meant for a short period to help you in times of difficulty, it was ever meant to be a way of life, living in that state day after day. My own body's response to fear was trapping me in a state where I was permanently on the lookout for danger. With the essence of time incredibly important to me, life began again in some dysfunctional way. Disorientated and jaded, I lived in an isolated world by myself. *15 minutes and I will be back in bed. That will only take me five minutes, I will be back safe in five minutes.* I would do the things I had to do, but they were on time scale and mentally, that was the only way I could approach doing them. Collecting the kids at 4pm was an achievement. It was an achievement to still be alive.

Everything was a tremendous effort. No words I write explain how hard doing the smallest of tasks had become for me. I had gone from working full time, a busy, hands-on mum, to having a negotiation with myself to get out of bed, and when I faced getting out of bed the 'high alert' zone kicked in even more. It went from being background music, always there, lurking, to full volume the minute any conscious thought of leaving my hidden world was forced upon me. Disorientated and jaded, I only connected to the environment I lived in by physical pain. It ran down my spine and burned my back, leaving a tingling sensation down both of my legs and in my feet. But was it real? I had started to question everything. If no one could see it, it wasn't true, was it? It didn't exist, I was making it up. Or it was in my world but not the real world. That was right, wasn't it? After all, that is what I have learnt from that night in A and E. If it wasn't there to see, it wasn't a real problem.

The pains came on slowly. Sometimes more noticeable than others. Days went by with varied amounts of discomfort. I suffered a lot after I had to venture out into reality. Chest pain was frequent, but pains in my limbs and bones from my hands to my feet became quite paralyzing. It hurt to move. I would sweat so much even though I was so very cold, and every time I went to the toilet I needed to go again.

My life became a pointless existence to me. I was not participating in it, just levelling through a game trying to keep myself alive day after day, like a character in a Nintendo game. I had to battle baddies, jump across gaps and try to make it to home before I was crushed by spikey boulders that fell from the sky. Everything was out to get me. I was merely the character being moved along by someone else operating the controls. I formed a strange routine, everything blurred, I could not control what was out of my hands, and everything was. I had lost any ability to rationalise. I was so disconnected from everything that I no longer had rational thoughts. No one knew how close I was to drowning I was. I was numb to everyone, just focused on the game I was in to try to make it out of this level alive.

Trying to control your thoughts when you have no rational behaviour is a somewhat impossible task. Every hour was spent hidden, apart from needing a drink and using the bathroom; living upstairs under a blanket was how I faced life. I began to grasp at elements to control, with time being the most tangible one. I had everything down to a minute. I noticed things that would reinforce fear. Things that would be overlooked in life's general terms, but that became big issues to me. As houses often do, we had a gate at the bottom of the drive. This gate served the purpose of keeping the dogs from escaping, but apart from that it was often pointless. On most occasions the dogs were nearly always kept around the side of the house, hence the driveway gates were often open. It caught my attention one day; walking back from the en suite I peeked around the blind as I heard a slight knocking. It was the gate in the wind. Open. Like it always was. Just knocking against the brickwork in the breeze. Seeing it opened wide like that made me panic. More than panic, it sent sheer fear down my spine. My safe world was open. It had to be closed and locked. I asked David to make sure in the morning he would close it on his way out. He did so without question. He seemed to have picked up on my new irrational behaviours: if he did want to question them, he never did. He just reassured me it would be locked and I would be safe. The unlocked gate was an opening to the world I could not control. A barrier in my defence was down, an opened crack where things could get me. There was no way I could go and close the gate myself. The act of stepping out the house to do that seems very simple, but for me, in that state of turmoil, it was a less evil task to worry and let my imagine run wild with thoughts of what could come through the gate rather than physically put myself at risk of being in that world even for a split-second to close the gate myself.

I sensed bad things. I was nervously on edge and riddled with fear. I began to trust my dog, Biscuit, more than myself. A fully-grown adult looked at her faithful hound to direct her through life. That is how disconnected my hold on reality had become. I could not trust myself. Every time historically I had hope, things got worse in life. Every time I thought I could handle things and had hope for an outcome of some sort I could manage, it was unfounded and I was proven to be stupid. My mind played tricks on me. I would manage to calm myself down just to have an unexpected bolt of out the blue that created more shock. It came to the point that I could not, would not trust my own feelings. I lived through Biscuit's intuition. I trusted him more than my own thoughts. He knew. We had this connection. He looked at me, his eyes at mine, and he seemed to understand. If he was agitated or unsettled, so was I. I would await his response if I felt nervous. I would watch his behaviours. If he was calm and settled, I was going to be OK. Biscuit knew.

I always heard the postman coming. We had gravel stones on the drive, and as soon as the gate was opened I would hear the footsteps coming towards the house. Then the dogs would start the barking from the kennels around the side of the house. By this time, the panic had already set in. The chest pains, the shortness of breath. Building and rising in intensity. The letters dropped on the doormat with the usual thud. Then the footsteps back on the gravel, down the drive. I would wait in anticipation of hearing the bolt on the gate being locked. Some days I heard it, some days I didn't. Those days were incredibly hard. Feeling vulnerable and unsafe if the gate wasn't locked, yet too scared to go out and close it myself. The postman and the gate became thoughts of panic. The postman, as nice as he was, represented a connection with the outside world. Bringing news and bills in the post, he provided a direct link to the world I no longer fitted into and the world I had manage to form some sort of existence in. Letters, no matter what they were, proved that although I did not fit in anymore in the society I once had, I could not escape it. The post caused me utter distress. The anxiety skyrocketed, the sound of the gate being opened, the humming of the postman. It was not just about the postman entering my sanctuary, it was not just about the gate being locked, it was about that connection with outside world, a reality I could not endure. A world of responsibilities, jobs, choices, decisions and things that only functioning, sound-of-mind adults can cope with. Bills had to be paid, car insurance policies had to be renewed. I had disconnected completely from living, so no panic about the actions I had to take hit home. Bills could wait, I wasn't phoning anyone to renew a policy or release payment. Life had to wait. It was the fact that I had no control of stopping life happening around me that I struggled with the most. I wanted life to stop, to pause, to wait whilst I came to; yet it kept on going.

We were lucky where we lived. Not many people called on the off-chance we would be in. Living rurally in a hamlet surrounded by fields, no one would generally drive at least ten miles out of their way unless they knew we would be home. That was a comforting thought. I had cut a lot of people off. I was so busy – busy working, busy with the kids. Who wouldn't know any different? Friends hadn't realized I had stopped working, stopped living. When work colleagues text me, I ignored them. When friends asked if we were meeting up for afternoon tea, I was busy. When family wanted to visit, I put them off, maybe next weekend. I could not bear to see anyone, and, with a lot of my closest friends and family living so far away, no one doubted my excuses at all. My bubble was protected. That's not to say nobody knew there was something wrong. I couldn't hide it from everyone but I had become a master of pretence on many occasions. Friends who noticed the most were the ones who had connections because of the children. David would collect the children from hobbies, it used to be me all the time. A social butterfly, I would interact with everyone, then suddenly I was no longer seen about. I would get messages asking if I was OK... haven't seen you in a while... the kids say you haven't been well. Delete. Ignore. I was intentionally cutting good, caring people of my life and I did not care. I had gone from being reasonably social, always messaging friends and family to see how they were, being there for them, letting them know I was there if they ever needed anything, to a total numbness towards everyone. Protecting myself by isolation in a world that I could barely survive in was the only way I knew how to live, how to manage and how to stay alive.

Half asleep under the duvet one day, I heard the gate open. Assuming it was the postman, I waited for the thud of the post landing on the doormat followed by the trudge back down the drive on the gravel stones. It never came. I was half asleep. I never slept well, more like a dazed consciousness of flashing memories, strong emotions, snippets of calm then dark deep moments of inner turmoil. Had I heard the gate? No, I mustn't have. The dogs weren't barking. I mustn't have. I could always look out and see if that royal mail red van was there. No. I must have been dreaming it. There was nothing but silence; the process of talking myself down from the high alert began. *It was nothing, go back to sleep. You're safe.* My heart raced, my breathing was shallow and I felt like a deer in the headlights even though I was hidden under a duvet and alone. Then the dogs started. They had heard it too. I wasn't going mad. There was a humming, and footsteps on the gravel. I froze under the covers. As if someone could see me, I played dead. I don't even remember breathing. This rollercoaster of emotions I had experienced within the last few minutes, the intense panic to trying to calm myself down, this was my life now. Hung up on every sound, assessing who, what, where, when the danger would strike. I heard ladders against the side of the house. I knew instantly who it was. The window cleaner. Now we all know; window cleaners are usually jolly folk who like to whistle whilst they work and never refuse a cup of tea. Well, mine was. An elderly chap who always loved to know the village gossip. What did I think of the new owners of number 2? Who bought that land heading up towards the forest? To say he lived a few miles away, he certainly knew more than I ever did about what was going on in the village. There was no way he would get offered a cup of tea, or get paid even. He was not welcome; he should not be here. For the first time, I felt angry. How dare he come past my gate, onto my safe land. This wasn't expected like the postman's visit. This has caught me off guard and I was angry, I was frightened and terror took a hold of me, all because of him.

Immobilized with panic and anger, I stayed where I was, hidden under the duvet, paralyzed with fear. His humming continued and the dogs stopped their barking. They must have recognized his tone, after all, I guess this bloke did come every six weeks or so. I was never in but he often called back in the evenings or at the weekend for payment. The dogs must have been satisfied it was the usual sound of a bloke who called every so often and settled down into the kennels once again. He moved the ladders. I heard the rubbing of the aluminium against the brickwork when he began to climb. He was near my window. The banging of him climbing the steps, the humming and then suddenly the noise of the window swisher right there, next to my bed. The bedroom window was covered. I had not opened the blind for a long time. I knew he couldn't see in but that did nothing to reassure me. I was at crisis point. Barley breathing, this person was invading my privacy, my only safe place. As he cleaned the window and polished them up, the sound of the cloth squeaked against the glass. His whole presence so close to me installed utter fear. Holding my breath in case he heard me, closing my eyes, longing for the moment to be over. Now I cannot remember him finishing and leaving, the sound of his footprints on the gravel nor the dogs barking. Hidden under my duvet, I passed out.

'I'm not looking for much else right now, just to heal.
To feel peace caress my skin and to make home underneath it'

S.C. Lourie

NOT ME, NOT I

Six glasses. Six glasses broken in one week. That's when I first realized the physical outward signs. Until then, it was all my best kept secret. I felt the chest pains, the aches, the immobilizing panic inside, but they were invisible to the outside world. Invisible meant they weren't real, or if they were only I knew about them. The broken glasses were the first external signs. No, it wasn't because I was clumsy or they were the finest more delicate cut glass, nor was it the porcelain sink which cracked glasses just by looking at them. It was me. Nervous, so very nervous and so full of fear. The world in my head hadn't just claimed my mind now, it was growing and claiming my body too. The world as I knew it, my world, the reality in my head, was showing its first signs of creeping through. The nervousness, the stammering, the clumsiness, the hyper sensitivity to noise; everything seemed so loud. The constant need for the toilet and the sweating. It had moved from my mind, my head, to my body, my speech, my hands.

One day I woke up and felt the need to do something. The room adjacent to our bedroom was effectively our spare bedroom, primarily for when Mum came to visit. In the meantime, it was a walk-in wardrobe for me, something I absolutely loved. My own space organized in my own way. Quite frankly, when we looked around the house pondering the purchase, the walk-in wardrobe was the selling factor for me! I lay in my bed feeling restless, agitated and annoyed. I thought about the wardrobe room at the back of the house. The window overlooked the fields only, no one could see me in there. I decided to go in.

Every time something bad happened in my life, I was wearing blue. Now it is fair to say I liked blue so I guess I did have a considerable number of blue items, but the colour filled me with fear. Blue was an omen; something bad would happen to me. Thinking back through the heartaches I had experienced, the trials of life, bad news, hospital appointments, hard times; I was always wearing blue. *When it happened.. I was wearing blue.* I could think of nothing positive that had happened to me whilst wearing that colour no matter how hard I tried. I wanted rid of it. Every item was to go. In my pyjamas, I went through my tops, my trousers, my sweaters, my jackets. Anything that made me feel uneasy went. It didn't matter if I liked them, whether they were relatively new or a not-so-recent purchase. A branded item or an off-the-peg sale bargain, it was to go. I produced quite a pile by the door, all those bad luck clothes. It felt good to see them, they were soon to be gone, out of my house, out of my life. All those bad moments with them. I ventured downstairs to fetch a bin liner. The house felt so big, so open, so exposed. All I had to do was get a large bag and return to the top corner room of the house. Where I would be, safe and hidden. The window at the bottom of the stairs, it got me every time. I felt vulnerable and unmasked seeing the outside world enter my home though that pane of glass. I dropped the venetian blind to cover it straight away, my heart pounding as I went to reach the cord pull, hands so nervous I could barely grasp the strings. World blocked partially. Yet the light still shone though the slates. Maybe someone could still see in, still see me? We needed a new blind, one of those black out ones. One that no one or thing could peak through. It was on a mental list to ask David to sort. Now I could get that bin liner and get back upstairs safe. Before I knew it, I had produced a bag full of blue. All shades, all ridden with bad news, bad feelings. I was exhausted, it was quite simply the most I had done in a long time. Everything was put back neatly: shoes lined up, everything in order. All I had to do was get rid of this bag. Now, normally I am a huge charity shop giver. But this bag couldn't go there, it had to be destroyed. This was good-quality clothing that would have come in useful for so many people, but I could not donate these to charity. What if the bad luck that I found in them was to be passed onto another person? More heartache, more sadness. No. These, however wasteful it sounded, were only fit for the rubbish bin. Left by the front door with a note on for David – 'For the grey bin.'

Now, I barely went outside. I had the school run to do in the afternoon, which was a programmable 15-minute slot I had somehow managed to get my head around. A duty, a job, there, back. I didn't think about it and I just did it with an increased heart rate, sweaty hands and a wish that the kids could come out quickly and on time, heaven forbid I saw anyone. Apart from that I would not go out. David would collect the children from hobbies, and as the weeks went on he became more and more encouraging for me to go with him and sit in the car. He looked sad these days. I noticed it. It was true to say he was doing more than he ever had done, not only working full time but pulling my share of the weight with the children now as well. We had one income coming in, which he was providing, and he was doing most of the work inside the house as well. Knowing him though, it was not that that made him sad. Tired yes, but his heart was breaking because the woman he loved did not exist anymore. This person I had become, this nervous, hidden existence I lived, was not that of his wife, the person he had fallen in love with. When he asked me to go with him and collect the children one evening, like he did every week, his face already knew my answer. His eyes looked heavy, resolved that once again he would be going on his own. Those blue eyes I had seen sparkle over the years were lost. A split decision. *Yes* If I had thought about it, it would have been an no. Do it quick I thought, go. Don't think. It was dark, he promised straight there, straight back. Before I knew it, I was in his car, still in my pyjamas, with his fleece on and my old dog walking hat. I was going out when I didn't need to. As he began to drive, we sat in silence as I stared out the window. I felt the fear intensify inside my chest. What if I saw someone? What if they wanted to speak to me? I shouldn't have left the house. It was a mistake, what was I thinking? The trees blew in the wind, darkness all around. I had nowhere to hide and felt so vulnerable seeing the world around me. Like he sensed it, David reassuringly took my hand.

When he pulled up in the car park waiting for our daughter to finish training, I felt paralyzingly numb with fear. I needed to get home. What a stupid decision to agree to come. The centre door was opened. People were beginning to leave and more cars pulled up awaiting to collect the youngsters. I secretly begged for her to come out, *come out now, quicker quicker, now*. I couldn't tell you what David was talking to me about, I just kept focused on the door. Every moment felt like an hour. What was I afraid of? People seeing me, wanting to talk to me, what would I say? What could I say? Brioni got into the car. Yet panic still overcame me. *Hurry up, Dave, drive, start the car. What is he waiting for? Come on, man.* Seeing people who could function, people who would wonder what on earth had happened to the woman they once knew, I felt intimidated, nervous and scared. By the people I once called friends, by the fellow human race, by anyone who could manage life. Psychologically maybe it was more about my own realization of not being able to function that scared me the most, that would be so visible next to anyone who could.

"Mum! I didn't know you were coming, why didn't you come on up?!' Everyone has been asking about you!"

"I I I I I will do another time, not n n n now."

"That's a shame. They always ask how you are you haven't been up in ages, Mum. People miss you."

Home, just get me home.

I had cut myself off from the outside world. I lived in a bubble that blocked out people, events, life. I knew it was all still going on around me, but I had no interest in playing a part in it. Messages kept coming; I lied and said I was busy. I was busy, but not in a way most people, no matter how much I liked them as friends, would understand. I was busy surviving, taking deeper breaths, busy telling myself I was OK, busy silencing irrational thoughts. Quite simply, I had never been as busy in my whole damn life.

There is a mirror on the landing, full length. Always great for those nights out, can match heels perfectly with any dresses and see how it looks without struggling and wondering if I have got the right pair on. I noticed how I avoided that mirror, any mirror.

My physical behaviour had changed. I looked down at the floor most of the time, avoided eye contact with anyone. I certainly looked down at the floor passing that mirror. Something to do with the identity of the reflection. It wasn't who I was.

The girl in the chair with the long brown hair. Well, that used to be me. A flirtatious smile and predictably wild, always trying to please. The girl I used to be has a terrible case of mistaken identity, and yesterday's girl is not what you see. Just a terrible case of mistaken identity.

That's not me, it's just not me. That's not me.

I had never been the sort of personality that demanded control or power. Not in any aspect of career or in my personal life. It was not my nature. Too soft, too sensitive and too easy going for any direct claim to power. Organized, yes, tight rein on my young children, possibly, out of protection but not for the love of domination. Yet it became apparent to me that I had absolutely no control, over anything. Not one thing. I could not control what happened at work now; the implications I faced due to my behaviour, I could not control the need to hide away, the opinion of my children on what had happened to their mother, nothing. Not the future I had once planned, the bucket list dreams, the ideas of adventures. Not that anything is promised in life anyway, but I had no way of even directing anything I once wanted to happen to take any formation. Not even on who could come up my driveway. I began to grasp at any control I could. Primarily, this was the mindset of I can choose when to die. If the next moment is too hard, the next hour, the next day, I could die then. That power of choice was clung to like a life raft at sea. It was the only thing I had. My choice to live or die at any given moment, and I gave myself a permission to go when I wanted. Subconsciously, however, I had another thing I could control. I didn't realize at first, but my eating habits had become something I had power over. What I ate and when I ate it. If I would feed this body of mine. That was down to me. I lost a lot of weight and quickly. Did I believe I was overweight? No, I didn't. But there was never any rational thinking as to whether I was or not. I had always wished to be more toned, firmer in certain areas when I was thinking straight, but now this didn't even come into it. It wasn't about the food. It was about the power I had over it and the feelings associated with grasping at some sort of thing I had a say in in my own life. I didn't deserve nice things, nice food. It was a punishment to myself above all else. I had always been a stickler for vitamins, making sure the children always had the appropriate ones, that their diet was supported with anything that was possibly missing. I couldn't justify taking mine anymore. A waste of a good little pill on me, useless, pathetic me. I'd see the little bottles left out on the kitchen side some days and I could not bear to look at them, never mind take one. Such low self-worth that a single multi-vitamin tablet was too much of a privilege that this waste-of-space body I had deserved. Born out of the lack of worthiness I felt to eat, and the control over what I could and could not do in life, I would go without food for days. I didn't deserve anything nice and I wasn't going to reward this failing body and mind of mine with anything. When I did eat it was guilt ridden, backed up with the thoughts of how I didn't deserve it. An unhealthy relationship with food had inadvertently developed, little did I know it was only making myself struggle harder with life.

David had listened, he bought a new blind for the downstairs window. He didn't understand what was wrong with the one we had. With references to 'The Twits', to remind me that windows are for looking out of and not in through, he tried to make light of my reasoning that the slates were letting the world in.

Anyway, he purchased one. It was a shade of blue.

IN MY OWN TIME

Mental breakdown, otherwise known as a nervous breakdown, is the general term for an acute, time-limited psychiatric disorder that manifests primarily as severe stress induced depression, anxiety or dissociation in a previously functional individual to the extent that they are no longer able to function on a day-to-day basis. Closely tied to psychological burnout, sleep deprivation, overload and similar stressors may combine to overwhelm an individual with otherwise sound mental functions. * Definition as stated from the WHO

That definition is supposed clarify what happened to me. The words don't do it justice, or begin to explain anywhere near like how it felt, how it's impacted my life or what it has left me dealing with. Not one bit. Yet, it's a statement that is supposed to summarize my actions, my behaviours and my reasoning during a deeply traumatic time in my life. I suffered a Mental Breakdown. What this doesn't care to divulge is what it really means to me who has been through it. During my breakdown, the days were long and fog-like but the years short. Life happened still but I was no longer a part of the world I once knew. It subsequently made me develop high-functioning anxiety. I lost interest in life and withdrew to a very dangerous level. My body/mind shut down to protect 'me' from something I could not cope with. Effectively trapped in an unlocked cage, suffocating. Worry is verbally focused whilst anxiety includes verbal thoughts and mental imagery, and this difference is important. Emotional mental images, such as those associated with anxiety, provoke a much greater cardiovascular response than emotional verbal thoughts. Worry triggers problem solving but anxiety does not – anxiety is a hamster wheel that doesn't lead us to productive solutions. The breakdown changed my behaviours. I became anxious about everything, I second guessed myself every moment, overthinking all things, losing the pleasure in life, mind and body refusing to co-operate no matter what you know is rational. Sweating, the muscle tension, the broken sleep and the chest pains. It was manifesting itself into a controlling eating disorder.

No matter what diagnosis someone receives, it is life changing. You may have that operation and make a full recovery, you may complete that course of chemotherapy and radiation, eventually reaching remission, but you change. You may fit back into the life you once had, you may have to change and make a new one. Illnesses, whether physical or mental. They change our course of life.

Medication takes its toll on you, whatever it is, whatever it is for. Someone told me once that when we become ill we must recover twice; once from the original illness, then from the medication we took for the illness. Doctors and consultants treat the diseases, physical and mental. But what about identity? Who saves that? Who helps us keep ours or helps build us another one when the one we've known gets destroyed? Medicine is the call to protect life, not merely life but the identity associated with that life. Another's soul. To help a person, medics must understand their patient's mind, his identity, his values. What makes life worth living and what devastation makes it reasonable to let that life end? To me, lack of hope was a reason to end my life. My breakdown took who I was and I lost all my identity. The saddest kind of sad is when the tears stop falling and you feel nothing. You don't cry, you don't hear and you don't see. For a second, the heart dies, but there is no emergency room that can save you, no CPR that can bring you back. You could be stood next to someone right now, sat opposite that man on the tube reading the Metro, and you could have no idea that person is dying before your eyes.

Breakdowns can happen for a variety of reasons, a combination of circumstances or following a traumatic event. Life left me isolated, waiting for everything to cave in, with just no idea of when or where it will happen and no power to stop it. Suffering then from anxiety and Post Traumatic Stress Disorder, I thought a lot about the impact anxiety has on us today. It is not just about a nervousness following something that has happened in life, like a fear of going outside and not being safe, it is powerful on a much more general level. Something I had never realised until my breakdown. Anxiety is the most prevalent psychiatric problem of our time. It is invisible yet life destroying. Constantly living in a high alert mode, waiting for some unknown impeding danger. Normal levels of anxiety are designed to protect us, a warning sign, but when it goes haywire what was meant to be helpful ends up paralyzing. In my opinion, the pressures of society today and the advances of modern technology intensify the problem, and I believe the epidemic of anxiety in young adults will only intensify. For example, the culture of now, connected to life 24/7, no time to disconnect, subconsciously impacts our mental health and wellbeing. Consider social media, for instance. Amazing benefits in communication no doubt, but think about the pressures of 'likes', the expectancy of instant messaging, needing an instant response... If not, when the blue ticks on WhatsApp show the recipient has seen and read the message but does not reply, what does that create in the person waiting? It gives way to irrational thoughts like: they are ignoring me; they don't like me; they don't like the idea; I've upset them. Now this may be farfetched to those who cannot comprehend the impact of anxiety, but to those who know what it's like, there are no rational thoughts of logic or of understanding that the other person could possibly just be busy when you've already overthought things and have a thousand different reasons why there is no response, or no like, or no comment. We are caught up in this frenzy searching for approval yet not from within. Years of education and yet many of us have never learnt to love ourselves. Social media pressures us to present our best to each other. Subconscious questions of 'who can I persuade people who I am' forcing us more to create the perfect identity for ourselves than to get to know the one that is deep within us.

High-functioning anxiety looks like busyness, achievement, perfection. It can sneak out in nervous habits, nail biting, foot tapping and stuttering. It feels like a punch in the stomach, paranoid stares, and it sounds like 'I am stupid', 'No one likes me', 'I'm not good at my job', 'I am a bad friend', 'I am not good enough'. Yet it appears perfectly calm. Looking for the next outlet.

Silent anxiety attacks hidden by smiles, overwhelming anyone with what could be the simplest of tasks. Destroying any peace, creating exaggerated reactions, confusion, lack of self-trust and fear. I didn't feel anything bar panic. It eats away, bringing about a slow and silent despondency to life. Creates a loss of polarity of judgement and leaves any sufferer with a lack of trust with everyone. My brain was overloaded and had short circuited, leaving me with absolutely zero confidence. I was nervous so often that I needed the toilet every time I left the bathroom. Stuttering, brain not engaging with body or sense. *Snap out of it, I would say, snap out of it.* But there was some sort of problem between my brain and my mind. My eyes wouldn't take in the information I saw, nothing would connect. I didn't ever want to wake up. I had a much better life when I was asleep. Living in a reverse nightmare, not waking up feeling relieved it was over, waking up and realizing it was my reality.

What I experienced through this breakdown is part of what some people suffer with for other apparent reasons. I am certainly not thankful, but possibly I was fortunate enough to have a trigger, a trauma that brought this about. When I say fortunate, it doesn't feel like that, but there is now something I didn't comprehend at the time that became a fundamental underlying reason that brought this shift in my life about. Something I could not find the words to say when I desperately needed help. Yet it is now something I can point too, something I can blame. Does that make it easier? Not one bit. Yet it helps to provide a reason, and a reason provides reassurance and comfort. I haven't found the guilt any less easy to deal with. In fact, I blame myself for it so like many people who feel or have felt this way. There is no comfort in blame when it is only directed at ourselves. What about those people who don't experience a trauma, those people who have mental health issues through no fault of their own? Bipolar disorder, split personality, those who battle clinical depression. Trapped feeling so low, so lost. Why should we isolate those who feel similar just maybe because of different circumstances? The desire of suicide has one thing in common that pulls whoever feels that way towards doing it: a lack of hope. So regardless of the diagnosis, it's the trigger, or the lack of one. Anyone who has felt that pull towards ending their own life has common ground.

The words that appear on my doctor's computer when he brings up my name say so very little about what I suffered with.

A Mental Breakdown. Attempted Suicide.

It doesn't say:

Chronic anxiety

Crippling fear

Smiling depression

Phobias

Extreme self-loathing and sense of hopelessness

Inability to sleep

Difficulty in concentrating

Clammy heads and sweating

Irregular heartbeat

Hallucinations, flashbacks

Headaches

Pains throughout my body

Tension

A poor relationship with food

Trembling, shaking, dizziness

And it certainly doesn't say:

Wanting to die so much, as I didn't feel worthy or capable of living

"Your heartache is someone else's hope. If you can make it through, somebody else is going to make it through."

Kim McManus

BELIEVE AGAIN

I was online browsing the news pages when a headline really struck me. 'Suicidal patient waited unseen in A and E for 80 minutes before he was killed after running into traffic.' Along with the headline there was a photo of a young man. My chest tightened as I clicked on the link, my heart went out to him. I read the story: failed NHS targets; he went unseen and left on his own accord, where he then committed suicide. It deeply saddened me beyond all explanation. The article went on to say that this young man was known for his mental health condition and that his mother had phoned the outreach number that afternoon as she was concerned about him. She was advised to take him to A and E. What reduced me to tears was knowing how desperate that poor man must have felt. I can't say I knew what had got him into that position, or that I can relate to any diagnosis he had, but I feel for him so much. He was desperate, and after showing so much courage going into the hospital to ask for help, I felt not only heartbroken for him and his loved ones but angry that he hadn't got the help he needed. It is easy to look for blame is so many situations. Pointing the finger often sets things straight in our minds: why it happened; who did what. But in this situation this gives little comfort to those who need it. Blaming the NHS for his death is not why I highlighted this poor man's story. As it stands, the article went on to say there had been an inquest and the multiple failings of the department not meeting waiting times or indeed implementing the policy for those who present with mental illness were highlighted and action taken. But what is most alarming and the reason I felt so strongly about this, is that 18 months after Nicky's death, the Trust in question were still to implement the policies that failed him.

Suicide is a global phenomenon in all regions of the world. Over 800,000 people die by suicide each year and that figure is not inclusive of those who attempt it and go on to survive. Millions of people are then affected by suicide bereavements every year, and in 2012 suicide was the second leading cause of death amongst 15–30-year-olds globally. *Information from the WHO

More apparent in recent years is the push to approach mental health awareness and implement strategies for people who are diagnosed with mental illnesses. But what about those who don't fit into a tick-box category? Those like myself, who experienced a trauma that triggered a reaction that spiralled into a breakdown. Isn't that more often the case behind any mental health diagnosis? The anxiety and depression that followed, wasn't that a knock-on effect of the event rather than a mental illness? Yet I now have the label of a mental illness on my medical records. I often think we are forced to fit in a model that is generalised and not personalised. How can we fit into a system when it's impossible to even fit into your own skin? It was important to me to tell my story about my breakdown without explaining what caused it. Some people may think that is unfair, but by me it was the only fair thing to do. Explaining what happened to me, my trigger is another story, one that some people may be able to relate to, others certainly not. Justifying my actions, my thoughts and my feelings based on what happened to me would bring about an unconscious judgement from you, and one that would take away the importance of the journey that the mental breakdown took me on. My battle with anxiety, that is relatable to so many people. What does it really matter what caused it? We all need freedom from others' perceptions, and writing for me has provided that. The life event that brought suicide to me as the only option could have easily been several things. So many different reasons, yet so many people arrive at that same place. Isolating those who got to that place by a different means, whether it be redundancy, bereavement, abuse, chronic illness or bankruptcy, would be to disconnect with so many people who have battled with living like I have. Whatever the reason, making inner peace with the circumstances, having faith that good does wait for us, hope: that's the foundation for any recovery.

Nicky's story touched me because it was very nearly my reality. Reading it in the news like that I felt for him so badly, and his family and friends. How on earth did they manage to cope with what happened? The fear and torment that must have surrounded his last moments. That poor soul. I had sat there in A and E wondering what I was doing, feeling like I didn't belong. There were people in severe physical need and there I was. I came as close to Nicky to walking out and doing something very similar, and that frightens me a lot. How many other people can relate to this, I wonder? How many other people have there been, who found the courage to ask for help and then didn't get it? How many others have committed suicide because the experience they had when trying to get some help only reinforced their view that they were worthless? I know from my experience, asking for help in that way, the only way I knew how to at the time, not only reinforced my suicidal thoughts, it reduced my self-esteem even lower than I thought was possible, and getting over that treatment was indeed another hurdle in my recovery from what initially broke me.

It took me a lot to write a letter of complaint about the service I received that night in A and E. Through anger on the day I read that news headline, I wrote a letter of complaint because I came to a point where I realized I deserved better, just like Nicky did. That is a hard thing for me to acknowledge, and it is an even harder idea for me to accept. I did what I was told, I managed somehow to find some strength to go there and I was let down by a professional who had years of experience in mental health. She missed all the signs of a mental breakdown. My feelings discredited as a bad day. I was not believed as I had not attempted anything; no police had to get me off any railway line nor talk me down from a bridge. I was disbelieved and that at what should have been the point of my lowest and beginning the recovery made me spiral into even lower depths. This is not about the failings of the NHS, nor that one person who failed in their duty of care to me; it is about survival and learning lessons so things can change for that next person who happens to find themselves in the situation I did. In a society where everyone is so much more aware now of the stigma of mental health conditions and we hear Government initiatives on the radio and television, 'it's good to talk', my story along with others is proof not only that invisible conditions go undiagnosed, but also the fact that a verbal account was not enough to activate any help for me. Cancer can often be invisible. Yet it is most feared and the

NHS have strict referral regimes within specific time periods. The sooner the diagnosis and start of treatment, the higher the rate of survival. Anxiety is like cancer, an invisible disease eating away at you, destroying you from the inside out.

Some individuals hold the belief that the act of suicide is cowardly. You may be reading this thinking just that thought, or you may have been there, to that point and remember how brave you had to be to still be here today. Whether it is cowardly is debatable. Individuals who tend to think of suicide as an easy way out hold the belief that people are not courageous enough to deal with the pain they are experiencing in life. An avoidance plan for if you mess up, a way of not having to face up to the reality. Yet, as unique as the causes for driving us to that state of mind are the individuals who find themselves thinking those thoughts. It does take significant courage and bravery to continue living when your entire reality is ridden with pain. Suicide is a tragic act of despair rather than a selfish act. I say that, having been at that low point and standing as a Christian in front of God, knowing full well it was a sin to take my own life. One moment of pain for it to all end. Despite opinions, from being there, I can tell you there is nothing easy about it.

Recently I was waiting for the train home with my son at Euston station in London. I didn't want to be there. In truth, I didn't want to go to London that day. I had always loved London, the big bustling city, fast-paced lifestyle oozing possibilities for any dreams. It had always been the land of opportunity to me. Central city was a world where dreams were made, and indeed came true on many occasions. I had passed that on to my son, I know I had. He was a Londoner through and through. Even though he had been brought up in some rural country hamlet miles away from any city life, the excitement of the Big Smoke pulled him as it once had done me. Yet these days, living with anxiety, it felt a different place. The crowds of so many people, the organizing and responsibility to get my son to his training on time. Tubes, trains, people, nowhere quiet to hide. What if I got lost? *Becki, you won't get lost, you know London like the back of your hand.* What if someone speaks to me? What if I have no battery left on my phone and can't get in touch with David? What if I lose my bag? What if there's a terrorist attack? What if, what if, what if…

It sounds easy and somewhat fun to have a day away from normal life, but when that anxiety takes hold it destroys everything. Yet I went, with the fear in my heart outweighed by the responsibility of a parent. Sometimes in life the fear won't go away, so we face things afraid. A day out with my son getting to see him doing what he loves, it was that thought that got me up and gave me the strength to go. Easy to write but not easy to do. I had got up early with an excited young man, delivered him safely to Saddlers Wells Theatre and sat by a tree in the park opposite with a big piece of cake; a treat to myself for managing it, for stepping out into that big wild world I often find so frightening. That was the best piece of cake I had ever had. I guess that is what is meant by living with anxiety but not letting it win.

I heard the news over the loud speaker that the train was going to be delayed indefinitely due to a death on the line. The sign of frustration and anger from the waiting crowd stuck me. Huffs and puffs, people immediately on their mobiles informing loved ones, friends, colleagues. No one seemed bothered about the person who had committed suicide, or their loved ones. It was a total inconvenience. I glanced around; people were back to their magazines, books, and phones whilst they waited. It meant nothing to them. Nights out ruined, missed connections, late arrivals and tired people who just don't have time for this. I looked around and heard snapshots of conversations, people sitting back down on the floor with their bags. Unhappy and fed-up expressions filled the train station departure lounge. A spokesperson announced the news again, offering apologies for the inconvenience caused. They will update us as soon as they can, thanking us for our patience in advance. I felt sick. I didn't want to be here anymore than the next person, but that wasn't the reason I felt my stomach turn. That person, whoever he or she was, they must have been at their most desperate point. That resonated with me. To have been at that point, to have felt that low and in need of a way out, I was deeply saddened that an individual near here tonight felt they had no choice but to escape life in that way. Whatever had drove them to it, the pain of living through their hell was more than enough to bear. With no hope left, those terrifying final moments of life were seemingly less painful than what they had to face in their reality of living.

Of course, it is only natural to be fed up with the frustration and impact it has on our immediate selves. No one really wants to be delayed in life, but at the end of the day I could go home. I could wait and get home and my life will still carry on as I know it. My family were still there, together, still as one. Everyone in that station that night would get home eventually. Life would continue, and in 24 hours' time I might make some comment about the inconvenience of the delayed train, but you know as well as I do that we wouldn't think about that person, not really. And if we did, most people would comment; selfish sod, holding everyone up only thinking of themselves, would we really pause and think about the anguish they went through or the families suffering that had only just begun? For so many people who knew that person, their lives would be changed forever. The pain and sadness that person who committed suicide felt hasn't ended, rather simply transferred to those around them. Unanswered questions maybe, no reasons, no peace and no chance to say what they had always wanted to. I had a three-hour delay; they had a lifetime of unexplainable heartache.

Whatever takes us to that option in life, whatever pressure finally forces us to that point is something I have spent a lot of time thinking about. For me, and I do believe a lot of others who have tried to kill themselves, the vision of life is that everything must be fixed. We are human and it is a failure not to fix things, not to have answers. Our expectations and society pressures of this modern age means that we are programmed unrealistically to fix things. That way of thinking, it reinforces our worthlessness, our fragility. If we cannot fix it, we cannot manage. Yet some problems cannot be fixed. Some situations cannot be resolved; some things cannot be answered or justified. Once we realize this compassion and kindness kicks in when we don't have the answers, there becomes the change of mindset, and with a change of mindset living is possible. After all, compassion doesn't say 'of course there's no answer to this', 'of course you can't go on', it whispers 'together we can get through this'. It persuades, encourages, reassures and supports.

That was one of the reasons I began to write. It started with reading. When you read, you belong in someone else's story. You're not alone. I had always loved to read but with the pace of life and the commitments I had, reading time was limited to the odd holiday we had. Running a house, working, ferrying two children all over the country: my hobbies weren't my own; they became watching my children enjoy theirs and that gave me more enjoyment than a book could, but I did miss that escapism. I started to read when I was hiding. In the early days, I was too tired to do anything or interested in engaging either, but as the months went on I was still hiding but looking for a distraction to take me out of the hell I was living. Books provided that. I could suddenly be transported into another world, I was someone else, a character in a life could imagine living and you know what? It provided a safe escape for me that I loved.

I would read most things, bar fantasy and crime thrillers – I guess they never appealed to me. I was living in a high state of terror. Looking back I guess leaving my own horror story to live in another wouldn't have done me any good. Romantic novels, biographies of climbers who have scaled Everest, anything that enticed me into another world, of hope, love, chance and opportunity. Now with the great technologies of our day, my Kindle meant I could do this from my hidden place. No need to go to the library or search Waterstone's for the book with the cover that catches my eye. Just a click away. I had never been a fan of this type of technology, it is no match for getting lost in the pages, feeling the printed sheets, like you're really stepping into another world. But I was thankful for it. It was a blessing and became all I needed. Books are by far the cheapest vacation you can buy. We all need fantasy to cope with the reality sometimes.

The idea of writing was something that happened without me knowing about it, some unconscious motion I found myself participating in. Reading transported me into another world only accessed by powering up my Kindle and selecting the book. On the carousel one day I noticed 'Memos', a little app to store notes. I used to use things like that all the time when I was working and juggling everything; not so much a need these days. That thought saddened me. I missed work, the busy timetable I once led. Guilt and sadness as a realization that I could not manage that anymore, the girl I once was, wasn't me now, and that hurt. What started was a grieving process for the person I had left behind. I missed who I was. I missed my friends and I missed my old life. I wanted to go back and be her, I wanted that life before this had happened to me, yet no amount of wanting would ever take me back. People attempt to or commit suicide for so many different reasons. Whatever reason or feelings behind the thoughts change people, we are not the same as we were prior to whatever triggered that in us, and that takes time to come to terms with and adjust to. I grieved for the old me. I wanted her back, that woman who could cope, could handle things, had resolutions, had hope. That painful process of wanting and grieving was tremendously difficult. A terrible case of mistaken identity. It took a long time to realize that the grieving for who I wanted, what I could no longer have was to be was a step forward.

I used the memo app to disconnect from the thoughts in my mind. I figured that if I had to log into the story I wanted to live in more than my reality, effectively, I could put my reality into the memo app, store it there; and that's what I did. How I felt, what scared me, word, phrases, quotes that I felt I could relate to. Anything at all that was part of the hell I was living went into that app. Putting them down on paper, or indeed a screen in this case felt strange. Sometimes I could open it up and see all the thoughts I had had, reading them would make me feel worse and remind me of what happened, pain and heartache, so I began to not read anything I put in there; it became just a 'dumping ground' for my reality. It was like I had provided a place for the thoughts and feelings to live, rather than in my head. They entered my mind, I felt them, then I put them on the page in the app, and they lived there rather than in my mind. I am not saying suddenly I had a quick fix for every thought I had, but over time the process of dumping them in the app became a way of life. Little did I know at the time I was writing my own story whilst getting lost in another. The frustration, the anger, the tears all were directed into a little app on a seven inch Kindle. It became part of my daily survival plan. Nothing changed, the curtains were kept closed, the alarm was still set for 4pm just in case I fell asleep and missed collecting the kids after school. I just had something else to do along with the reading.

Day by day though, slowly and unnoticeably there began to be a change. A change in how I felt yet the reality stayed the same. I didn't suddenly wake up and feel better. Breakdowns don't work like that. The change that was happening was the first step in rebuilding me. I had got to that point where I was ready yet unaware I had started on a pathway offering some sort of recovery. Those dark days when I disconnected from everyone around me, I was totally isolated. It was my reaction to life to shut down and protect me. At that point, I could not even pray to God. I wouldn't say I have been highly religious nor totally committed the idea of faith. When I was a child I battled with the idea of religion. My parents used to drive my sister and I to the local church at nine am on a Sunday morning and drop us off, only to come back at lunchtime and collect us. They wouldn't come in and attend the service, yet it 'would do us good'. I often wondered about this. Wouldn't the best lesson to have been to watch my parents show us faith and lead us instead of delivering us to church for some sort of daycare under the pretence of having a solid grounding of Christian ethos instilled in their children? My parents' misinformed idea of bringing us up with Christian morals and guidance was a lesson never taught no matter how many services we attended over the years. 'Drop and Go' is not a way of incorporating religion into family life, yet I guess it may ease conscience and provide some sort of reassurance that their children would have moral grounding. My grandparents, whom were Salvation Army members and I loved seeing them get dressed in the uniform and go off to the services. That was a separate world. Sometimes we would go to special occasions and be introduced as Brigadier Mitchell's grandchildren, where we would smile and look pretty, sit straight and be well behaved, but religion and God were most distance at those times. I grew up with the notion of religion but not ever being a part of it, and never feeling it. It is true: when we get bad news or something goes wrong, we immediately pray to God, whom we have ignored for most of our lives, for a miracle to help save us from what we face. Reading this you may remember a time you have done that, I know I have. When I fell pregnant with my first child, there were problems from the offset. It's funny, you never realize how much you want something, how much we take things for granted, until you risk losing it. One evening I was taken to hospital and was told the next few hours were most important to see if my baby would survive or not. When the nurses left me in the side room, I cried so much and begged the Lord to save my unborn child. Looking back now, I hadn't prayed for years before that. I begged God to save him. We were incredibly fortunate and my son was born a few months later healthy and happy. We called him Zac, which means 'remembered by God'. I thought it was fitting as God had remembered him that night, I truly believe that is the only reason he survived. Yet reflecting back now, did I become more committed to religion after Zac was born and go to give thanks? I had faith, but I did not act on it. I incorporated it into my family's life by saying grace at the table and other gestures, but I never felt a strong connection. Life took over, God was there, he helped me when I prayed, I was thankful, then it got pushed to one side. Not forgotten about, just moved over whilst on the highway of living, life sped up. That's how life went on. Maybe you can relate to that. It sounds very shallow, very wrong to use someone for what they can give you without giving anything back, and although that was never my conscious intention, it was my action.

Ironically that night, that evening in A and E, I could not pray. I felt no connection or an openness to deserve it. I sensed no presence of God. I could not pour out my heart to him. He had seen what had happened, what I had tried to do, he would have seen it all and heard all my thoughts. I was ashamed. I had no worth. I was guilty, lost and I truly believed God would not help me, not this waste of space I had become in life. God was blocked out. Entirely, from that moment on. I deserved nothing, I was taking up valuable air that someone else more worthy could be using. I made myself as small as possible, even in my own bed, to take less space upon this earth; who was I to even exist here, never mind live? I cannot sit here and say that the night in A and E was as low and dark as it got, that it was an upward journey from then on. It hasn't been by any means that simple. It got darker than that night. My mind travelled deeper under those covers at home to edges of reality I never knew existed, where I was totally isolated, alone and disorientated.

A mental breakdown can only be described as a storm. A grade five collection of hurricanes that hit fast and hard, wiping me off my feet with no chance of weathering the gale. Before I knew it, I was disorientated, disillusioned and even when the winds died down and I recognized where I was once again, standing up on my own feet I still felt the motion of the movement, like that sea-sickness motion you feel once you've left the boat and are standing on dry land. Things linger. Effects of the aftermath and the coming to terms with the hit can sometimes be more difficult than the initial blast. Whether you walk into the storm knowing you face a challenge or it hits you from behind, the attack brings fear, grief, pain and hurt. I felt utterly alone and lost. Unreachable by everyone. Trauma leads inevitability to a shift that interferes with how we interact with ourselves, others and the world around us. It was when I was facing the eye of the storm that I realized God walks towards us to meet us in the middle of the carnage. He wasn't walking alongside me, he met me in the thick of it face on, and that was when I felt glimmers of courage, trust, hope and faith. Somehow and in one of those days spent hiding from life, God entered purely and unbeknown to myself at that time, something reached out to me. And for that, I am eternally thankful. Hand on heart, God is the only reason I have made it this far. In him I did find a place of safety. What was noticeably different from anything I had ever experienced before, was I didn't reach out to him, but him to me. In my search for peace I found that spirituality was a saving grace.

God wanted me to trust him one day at a time. He didn't want me to be concerned with tomorrow until tomorrow. You know what I realized? I realized that I missed out on the now. Looking back at my life, I had always missed out on the 'now'. The first step for me was taking that overwhelming pressure off myself. One moment, one minute, one hour, one day at a time. Focus on today.

For some reason I was pulled back to my memo. I felt a draw to it. The ever-growing list of words and random sentences that were written, there was a strong yet painful connection I couldn't get away from. I had an overwhelming urge to write and tell my story, in actual sentences not just random thoughts and feelings. Ironically enough, when I read and tried to get lost in a story, becoming that character, something inside me was calling me back to my memos, and for the first time ever, I wanted to be a part of it. I had become comfortable with the word 'suicide', what it meant, its control, its escape. Being comfortable gave me the power to discuss it, think about it. Face it with compassion not fear. I guess the weight of mortality never gets any lighter, but it has got more familiar. Familiar meant comfortable, and comfortable meant I had compassion and empathy to tell my story. Now, I am no writer. To be honest, I can't spell that great and I am certainly not up with all the nouns and adverbs used in descriptive writing, but something told me to do it regardless. What I did have were feelings, experience travelling into some very dark destinations and a vision to reach out to others. I doubted my ability constantly, and my doubt became my passion, and my passion became my task. I told myself to write, regardless. Tell your story.

Not just for me, for people like Nicky Sullivan. It is sadly too late for him, but not for others.

*"Dearly beloved, we are gathered here today
to get through this thing called life."*

Prince

RIGHT HERE IN MY HEART

Living is indeed the hardest part. Life is not easy. The trigger that took me into the hospital that night will never leave; it is part of my life, my story. I look back at my life and I am really surprised that I am still alive. If someone had told me then that I would be here now, they couldn't have been further from the truth at that point in time. What I can tell you is after suffering a mental breakdown and attempting suicide, I am a new person. Not who I was, a new me with a different perspective. Now I notice things and can appreciate more now than ever before. I didn't just wake up one day and say, 'You know what, I think it's time for me to be happy again.' It was never as easy as that. It took time, and still takes time to this day to allow myself to feel worthy of being happy, and accept who I am and what happened. But I found a way through, not with tablets nor counselling, just with an approach to life, literally taking one day at a time. I still remember the days I prayed for the things I have now, to be able to smile, to go outside and enjoy the breeze on my face. I longed for them, and I make a conscious effort to remember those times because it is easy to forget. And you know what I've learnt more than anything? That happiness comes from within. Life is never perfect: there are fleeting excellent snippet moments, but only if we notice them. We wait for everything to fall into place; work, family, love life, financial security. It is very rare and often impossible for all these things to be in tune with one another, and I have been guilty of wanting this. There are so many special moments to be had, if we just stop, accept things in life will always be beyond our control and just appreciate the moment, we would be so much happier. Since my breakdown, I notice so much more and feel so much more. I see the joy in people's eyes when they tell me their good news, I notice the sun shining on the garden and see the flowers. I feel the excitement of doing something I had dreamed about. I don't take anything for granted, and most importantly I feel the freedom to live and accept who I am, what I have done good in life, what I have done badly and notice things. I notice the world around me now on a deeper level, and for that I am thankful. It has only been through this mental illness that I have realized how beautiful my world it. Not perfect, but truly beautiful.

I've also had to face some awful things. Appearing in court, hearing news I never wanted to hear, holding my hand up to my own bad choices and errors, falling back into things I promised myself would never happen again. It is not a walk in the park by any means. Life isn't easy. It never has been or was before. What a mess I have made since the breakdown and after. I am no angel, I've seriously messed up. I mess up on a daily basis actually. But I look at all the things I would have missed. My daughter's birthday, seeing her eyes light up with excitement. Not being there to help her when she was upset about friends at school. Who would have really seen she was hurting when she just says 'I'm fine'? My son's appearance on that big stage, telling him it is all OK before he went in for his heart scan. Those little things, those things are my world and I am so thankful I didn't miss out on them now.

It's funny now but when I was writing I often listened to music. One artist in particular related to me, the lyrics from her songs resonated, and there was feeling from the piano that said more than the words. The artist I was listening to had just released a new album and was putting together a tour. I often wondered what it must be like to produce your own story through music and connect with people. Then I realized I was doing my version of that with my writing. Her drive and passion encouraged mine. Especially on the bad days. And still now there are days I just cannot participate in life; it can be so overwhelming. Just because a person smiles all the times doesn't mean their life is perfect. That smile is a symbol of hope and strength. So many things, so many days when everything is too much and I worry about slipping back into that existence that took hold of me. It is never too far away and if I run away with life and feel the heaviness and the weight of it, it can get me down. And that is where my approach of taking each day as it comes has helped. I stop and listen to music, I simply connect again to me. Life is a constant invisible battle for people riddled with anxiety. Whether it be that job interview we have just been for, the worry about an little impending arrival, how the bills are going to get paid at the end of the month, or major concerns for me like having to leave the house... Worry steals today's happiness, and those moments are far too precious to lose. Accepting the feeling, acknowledging it is there, saying hello and saying goodbye to it. It becomes manageable and something we can live alongside not under its control.

Still to this day I….
- Struggle
- Am afraid of the colour blue and am reluctant to wear it
- Dislike magpies and worry what will happen… I panic, what bad thing is wait for me next?
- Have moments of longing for my bed and my blanket when I am finding life hard.
- Hide under the duvet when I need to
- Wake up and worry about going out of the house and seeing people
- Dislike window cleaners!
- I am still weird around people and feel uneasy sometimes.
- Make mistakes and blame myself repeatedly for them.
- Panic about things.
- Overthink.
- Avoid mirrors – struggle with identity, image of me and what doesn't match up to that inside.

Some things that help me live...
- I pray.
- I look for signs. I ask for signs. They reassure me and give me guidance. Feathers, rainbows, robins. They offer me a sense of connection and promote an inner peace.
- Looking forward to the little things – telling myself about them. Hot chocolate and a blanket when I finish work. Not having to leave the house tomorrow.

- Some old-fashioned things like fresh air are hard to beat. I take a walk.
- I try and tell the negative committee that meets inside my head to sit down and shut up for a while.
- I accept myself. How I feel, I take pressure off and stop guilt tripping myself into pulling myself together immediately.
- I talk, I speak up and say how I feel
- I allow the feelings to come – I accept I want to go to bed and hide. I negotiate with myself, so I can do that, but not at this moment in time. Not when it interferes with living. I put things in place, and if I do those things and if I still feel like I need to do that initial reaction to my safe zone, I can.
- I write. I write about what hurts. I get them down out of my head onto paper. This acknowledgment stops me suppressing what I don't want to feel.
- The most important one... I give myself a break. I'm human. Admitting that life can suck and that I don't have to like it.

Remember you don't owe anyone an explanation for...
- Your level of education
- Where you live
- Your appearance
- Your political views
- Your belief in God
- Your alone time
- Your life choices
- How you feel
- Your bad days

You are you, how you deal with the journey you're on is unique and deserves no justification. That's freedom right there.

Daily reminders

- The past cannot be changed so never be defined by it. It was just a lesson, not a life sentence.
- Opinions don't define your reality. Identify the opinions in YOUR life that matter.
- Struggling doesn't make you a burden, or unloveable or undesirable or undeserving of care. It makes you human, and that does not discount your worth as a person. You can still be difficult and still be cared for, you can be less than perfect and always still deserving of compassion and kindness.
- It is OK not to be fine. You don't need to hold yourself together, and you don't need to pretend life is grand. Forcing positivity all the time is draining. Give yourself a break, be honest to you. Take that pressure off.
- Good hearts sometimes make bad choices, and use bad methods. Understanding that requires compassion. You are just as worthy of compassion as someone else.
- You can entertain a thought without accepting it. That's a real educated mind, and that doesn't come from school.
- Give up the need for control – try to allow everyone to be and everything to be just as they are.
- Never underestimate the power of a good morning text, an apology, or a random compliment, giving them is just as nice as receiving them, try it.
- Everyone journey is different.
- Sometimes fear won't go away, sometimes you must do it afraid. It is OK to be frightened.
- Make sure your worst enemy is not living between your own two ears. Listen to what you're saying to yourself. Would you talk to your best friend like that?

- Kindness is free, showing it to others helps your inner peace.
- Positive thoughts create positive things.
- Don't be in a rush to figure everything out, it is ok to embrace the unknown and let life surprise you.
- Overthinking will lead to sadness.
- Things get better with time.
- Allow each moment into your life, experience and touch it. Smell the flowers you just walked past and didn't even notice.
- You only fail if you quit.
- Let life pain visit, allow it to teach you but do not allow it overstay.

I haven't gone back to how I was. I have changed. Like a broken piece of crockery, you can glue it back together where it's cracked, but it is never the same. There is a custom in Japan called Kintsugi, which means 'golden joinery'. It refers to the art of fixing broken ceramics with gold. Cherishing the imperfection of the broken pot, it becomes a creative addition, a rebirth for the pot's life. A vessel fixed by Kintsugi will look more gorgeous, more precious that it was before it was fractured. There is a new 'me' now. Facing my own death, I struggled to rebuild my own life. Who could, or should I be? Perhaps it was never about rebuilding the old one, more about finding a new one. Once you look differently at the grieving process of what you've lost in yourself, you realize that you've gained something. Scary at first, unwelcomed and hated. Yet now I am stronger now in different ways that before, I notice more and feel deeper. I love more sincerely and appreciate things far more than I once did. I am OK with the new person this journey has changed me into. I put my broken pieces back differently. I have hope for the future now and, through faith, I have gained acceptance from the past, from what happened, and feel I can move forward most days. Some days win of course. Some days fill me with fear. Living consumes me I am flooded with nightmares of where I have once been and ever going back. Yet there can be beauty in tragedy. It has the power to motivate the human mind, and it can turn a weakness into strength and become greatness.

Wisdom is little more than healed pain so my advice for those who find themselves feeling similar pain would be -

Take life a moment at a time.

Do not think about the future, the next day, the next hour or even the next half an hour.

Focus on managing the minute you're in.

That's control and you still have it.

Stay connected. Feel your feet on the ground, take your shoes off to feel grass underfoot. Hold onto the stairwell and feel the smooth wood under your fingers. Smell. Listen. Taste the flavour of the coffee. Think about the texture on your tongue. Focus on something here, now, something real. Getting back on track is the biggest achievement. No matter how small a step you take. Sometimes that track is just remembering where you are and acknowledging it.

Get distracted from your reality, whatever situation that is playing on your mind 24/7. If you can't face a book, and believe me I couldn't at first, then music. Put some music on. Anything – the radio, it doesn't matter.

Remember... because YOU are alive, anything is possible. Anything at all. That's focus, and it's still there even if you can't sense it.

You may feel like you have no control, no way out? No way of sorting out this mess you find yourself living in? At any given moment, you have the power to say that this is not how the story is going to end. You can leave it like it is right now, and it will always be that way. Or you can stay and write on that blank page of tomorrow – an ending YOU can choose. That's control YOU have. Forces beyond your control can take away everything you possess except one thing, your freedom to choose how you will respond to the situation.

Trying to apply perspective to what you're going through is an incredibly hard task. But we must try. Change the view of yourself, a victim or a person who has grace and strength and can handle challenges. You are of course the later, as you're a survivor, reading this book. When you realize you can handle it, then you become the hero of your own story. Write how you feel. Words, sentences. Write down the negative thoughts and get them out. I assure you, screwing up those pieces of paper tomorrow when you have survived the night is a feeling you want to feel.

Stop thinking you're lost. You're not lost. Your own a road with no destination in sight just yet, driving with the hope you will get there. You're not lost. You're on your way. Like a car on the motorway, that vehicle needs maintenance, pit stops, refuel, the air in the tyres. It won't get there without it. Your body, your mind is the same.

Hope. Sometimes that's all you have when you have nothing else. If you have it, you have everything. Think of the next few minutes only. What can you give yourself to look forward to? A hot chocolate? What would you like if you make it through this? Grant yourself a wish. When you have it, whatever it is an hour or a day later, boy will you enjoy it.

Eat. Do I sound hypocritical yet? A cracker, a Hobnob. Anything. You are facing your biggest challenge of your life, and although you don't recognize it, you need fuel to help you get through it. Same for a climber leaving base camp for Everest – you need fuel for the challenge ahead. (And for those of you now thinking… wow Everest, that's a real challenge, what I am going though is nothing in comparison – you're wrong. You're fighting to live. That makes Everest a walk in the park.)

I am not going to tell you to try and have a good day. Instead, I simply want to advise you to have a day; stay alive, feed yourself well, wear comfortable clothes and don't give up on yourself. It will get better. Till then, just have a day.

You may be hurting now so bad. But what you can't see at this moment is that through this heartache, for the rest of your life you will be able to deeply understand the suffering and pain of others. You can use that gift to help others, that makes you a gift.

You have the strength to do this. I know you do. If you can hold that courage to make it through a lonely night with nothing but self-destructive thoughts for company, you can make it through anything.

I didn't want to do it alone. My story is not to promote battling away by yourself or not trusting people. Neither is it about promoting a non-medication route. Not at all. I wish my story had been different from that night. I wish I had got help, in any form when I needed it. Quite possibly some medication could have helped me, or some sort of counselling. The knock-on effect from that night I strongly believe caused me further problems, as I then had to deal with the breakdown and the perception that for whatever reason I did not warrant any help. My message to you is to ask. I still believe in asking for help. I still have hope that through journeys like mine, services for people will improve. That is the reason I wrote this, you're the hope I have for finding a way though. Ask and be honest about how you feel. After all, people start to heal the moment they feel heard. Try to be heard; your story will help others.

You may be screaming at me for this one, and right now it may seem wrong to think, but try to remember all of this is temporary. Whatever has got you to this point. All of this is temporary. It will pass and you need to be here to see that. If you're sitting there reading this thinking no, my chronic illness isn't temporary, no, my grief for my wife isn't temporary then yes, you would be right, at this moment in time right now. What is temporary is how your mindset sees that now. Give yourself the chance to change that; after all, if we can't change the situation, we can come to change how we view it. If you can't make something perfect, you can still make it beautiful.

What I want to tell you is that you deserve to live. You deserve to be. You are not a burden. The world needs you. Those thoughts, don't trust them, let it pass, like a wave on the shoreline. You don't need to take that thought and keep it, let it leave.

I don't give a damn if you are a CEO and hold conferences every morning, a hedge fund manager with a team of 50 waiting on your decision, a staff nurse, a checkout assistant or a teacher with an impending Ofsted visit. You are more than just a role, a responsibility and you're not fighting to stay in that role, you're fighting to stay you. Nothing is more important than YOU right now.

Since that night, it has been a journey of intense growth and facing my fears. That night I wanted nothing more than to end my life, convinced that everything good had gone. Time has moved on and now I am the future I never thought I would be here to see and in the same time I have managed to write my version of events to somehow make something positive out of a very dark time in my life. I have managed to get through the breakdown and I am beginning to stand again. I complained for the next person, for that poor soul feeling so lost right now. Someone somewhere will be feeling the same way I did that night, and if they have the courage to go and ask for help, they should get it. We should not have to prove how we feel to be taken seriously, we should not be judged on an image as to what we hide inside. I complained for all the people out there that feel they cannot go on and can't see how to live anymore. If a positive can come from my story, the next person who asks for help could be saved. I didn't complain for me, I complained for your friend, your family member, the next individual who walks into A and E. Possibly for you.

I have learnt to love the new year period. Nothing changes in a day, that strike of midnight doesn't magically make life better stepping out of one year and into another. I believe that thought alone can heighten depression, when the realization comes crashing down in the mist of January that we still have the same issues that bothered us a few weeks before. But there is a magic feeling that the prospect of a new year brings. The possibility of something new, something better, the idea of hope and how life can change, you can change, reality can change. Maybe every day is like that for some people. For you, I hope it is, but for me, that someone who couldn't look a minute ahead, to finding a time where possibilities feel real, hope feels real, that is magic. Whenever I think of the dark place I found myself in during that time of my life, I now focus and appreciate the one before me, how my mindset has changed yet still a work in process, and for the first time with excitement of what hope could bring, for that future I once did not want nor knew how to face.

If I could help someone through this I could save a life. What an achievement it would be to use my pain and make it into something worthwhile, something meaningful, something of hope. I realized I don't have to be an amazing doctor, a skilled surgeon or a firefighter to do something that could save a soul. I can offer myself; that is enough. Something as simple as reaching out and relating to someone so they don't feel alone. This was my driving force behind my vision. What if this hell, this battle I endured could help someone else? Suicide isn't talked about enough. My wish in life is for that to change. We talk about cancer, we talk about heart disease, Parkinson's and dementia. We feel for those who get taken down by illness outside their control. Yet suicide is still something society tries to banish: the shame, the guilt, the failure. No one ever asked to feel that way, and it doesn't matter how you reached that desperate point, or your friend, your colleague from work or the relative you love dearly; no one asked to feel that way. Just like the person queuing in front of you at the checkout didn't ask to be in need of a transplant, dependent daily on a machine to live, or the woman sitting opposite you on that park bench never wanted to live with an incurable chronic leukaemia.

I don't care how you survive, just so long as you do.

And you will, if you take life

One Day At A Time

"I hope one day you will find a peace, not in a place, but within you"

U.Rani

———

NO CRY FOR HELP

*I'm a therapist and I keep this poster in my waiting room.
Apparently, it's saved a few lives.*

*I don't like the phrase 'cry for help'. I just don't like how it
sounds. When someone says to me, 'I'm thinking about suicide,
I have a plan, I just need a reason not to do it,' the last thing I see
is helplessness.*

*I think: your depression has been beating you up for years. It has
called you ugly and stupid, pathetic and a failure. For so long you
have forgotten that it's wrong, you don't see anything good in yourself
and you don't have any hope.*

*But still, here you are, you've come over to me and you've banged on
my door, you've waiting for your appointment and said,
'Hey, staying alive is really hard right now, just give me something
to fight with. I don't care if it's a stick, give me a stick and I can
stay alive.'*

How is that helplessness? I think that's incredible. You're like a marine; trapped for years behind enemy lines, your gun has been taken away, you're all out of ammo, your malnourished and you've probably caught some kind of jungle virus that's making you hallucinate giant spiders.

And you're still going, saying 'Give me a stick, I'm not dying out here.'

A cry for help makes it sound like I'm supposed to take pity on you, but you don't need my pity. This isn't pathetic. This is the will to survive. This is how humans lived long enough to become the dominant species.

With no hope, running on your nothing, you're ready to cut through a hundred miles of hostile jungle with nothing but a stick, if that's what it takes to get you to safety.

All I'm doing is handing out sticks.

You're the one staying alive.

ANON

AGENCIES WHICH PROVIDE SUPPORT AND INFORMATION

SupportLine   **TELEPHONE HELPLINE:** 01708 765200
                     EMAIL: info@supportline.org.uk

Calm   **TELEPHONE:** 0800 585858
                     WEBSITE: www.thecalmzone.net

                     *Campaign Against Living Miserably Help and
                     support for young men aged 15–35 on issues which
                     include depression and suicide.*

HopeLine UK   **TELEPHONE:** 0800 068 4141
                     WEBSITE: www.papyrus-uk.org

                     for practical advice on suicide prevention

Premier Lifeline **TELEPHONE:** 0300 111 0101
                     WEBSITE: www.premier.org.uk/lifeline

                     *Helpline providing a listening service, information,
                     emotional and spiritual support from a
                     Christian perspective*

Samaritans   **HELPLINE:** 116 123
                     (free of charge from a landline or mobile)
                     EMAIL: jo@samaritans.org
                     WEBSITE: www.samaritans.org

                     *24 hr helpline offering emotional support for people
                     who are experiencing feelings of distress or despair,
                     including those which may lead to suicide*